Easy-Prep Lessons

More Toddlerrific

Fun Faith-Builders

David C Cook

transforming lives together

MORE TODDLERIFIC!
Published by David C. Cook
4050 Lee Vance View
Colorado Springs, CO 80918 U.S.A.

David C. Cook Distribution Canada
55 Woodslee Avenue, Paris, Ontario, Canada N3L 3E5

David C. Cook U.K., Kingsway Communications
Eastbourne, East Sussex BN23 6NT, England

Written by Jodi Hoch
Cover Design: BMB Design/Scott Johnson
Cover Photos:
        Boy: ©iStockphoto.com/Thomas Shortell
        Girl: ©iStockphoto.com/Ekaterina Monakhova
Interior Design: Helen Harrison
Illustrations: Nancy Munger

ISBN 978-0-7814-4561-0

First Printing 2007
Printed in United States

4 5 6 7 8 9 10 11 12 13

050509

Contents

INTRODUCTION 5

What to Expect from Toddlers 6

Setting Up a Toddler Classroom 8

Toddlers on the Grow: The Developing Mind 10

Toddlers on the Grow: Social and Emotional Development 11

Toddlers on the Grow: Developing Language 12

Prepare to Teach More Toddlerific! 13

ALL ABOUT GOD

1. Baby Jesus (Christmas) 15

2. Jesus Lives (Easter) 23

3. God's Promises (Noah's Big Ark) 31

4. Jesus Is Powerful (Jesus Calms the Storm) 39

ALL ABOUT GOD AND ME

5. Lost and Found (The Lost Sheep Is Found) 47

6. Talk to God (Samuel Talks to God) 55

7. God Is with Me (Moses Floats) 63

8. Follow God (Jonah and the Giant Fish) 71

ALL ABOUT GOD, ME AND OTHERS

9. Jesus Cares, I Care (Jesus Washes the Disciples' Feet) 79

10. Loving Others (Friends Show Love on a Rooftop) 87

11. God's Family (Zacchaeus in Jesus' Family Tree) 95

12. Helping Hands (Ruth Helps Naomi) 103

BONUS! "What I Did Today!" Take-Home Reproducible for Parents 111

INDEX 112

Introduction

Welcome to *More Toddlerific!* Similar in style and format to *Toddlerific*, this book is packed with fresh insights, new engaging activities, different Bible stories and updated trends in toddler development.

Are you ready for wiggling, squirming, poking, tumbling and nonstop action? This is the world of toddlers. They learn by doing, by playing and by exploring their environment. They soak up everything around them like little sponges. They move through emotional, social, physical and mental stages of development. They also move through stages of faith development. *More Toddlerific!* gives you 12 new Bible lessons that help toddlers learn about God. Each lesson helps you create concrete activities that will prepare toddlers to experience the touch of God.

At the end of each lesson is a page to send home with the parents called "At Home in the Faith." This page equips parents for their journey in being the primary teachers and builders of faith in their children. The "What I Did Today!" reproducible at the back of the book is a bonus parent piece that can be sent home whenever you choose.

"Toddlers on the Grow" will help you become more knowledgeable about toddler development. Toddlers and two year olds are often grouped together in church nurseries or Sunday school rooms. But an 18-month-old child is very different from a 28-month-old. These months are full of developmental leaps and bounds.

So get ready to wiggle—and grow the faith of your toddlers!

WHat to Expect FROM Toddlers

Toddlers are predictably unpredictable! One minute they are playing and the next minute they are crying. You are sure to see a myriad of emotions in a toddler classroom. As diverse as their behavior can be, toddlers do tend to exhibit some common behaviors. Remember, toddlers have limited language skills. They don't have the words to express themselves, so many behaviors are displays of frustration. Here are a few common behaviors, but more importantly, a few tips on how to deal with those behaviors.

CRYING: Many children cry. Crying may be communicating many different things, such as not getting their way, pain, fear, anger, separation anxiety, hunger, fatigue and frustration. Stay calm; try soothing the child and reflecting what you see. Say something like, "I see you are upset ... I know it's hard when Daddy leaves."

AGGRESSION: Children usually don't use aggression to be mean. They simply don't have the words to express what they're feeling or needing, so they take matters into their own hands ... or feet ... or teeth.

ME GENERATION: Toddlers are very self-centered and possessive. This is not very conducive to many social skills, such as sharing, but it is normal toddler development.

ATTENTION SPAN: Toddlers' attention spans are very short. They usually cannot sustain one particular activity for very long. They tend to move from one thing to another, leaving a trail of destruction behind them.

Dealing with Toddler Behaviors

There are no hard and fast rules or quick fixes in dealing with toddler behaviors. The following is a list of tools you can use from a "behavior toolbox." Depending on the behavior, you might need to reach in and use one, two, three or ten tools to help you in "fixing" the problem.

Use the power in the positive. Make statements in a positive way. State the behavior you want to see. If Cody is running around, then point out the child who is making a good choice. Say, "I see Jaymee sitting on the floor." This directs your attention to the behavior you want, not the misbehavior.

When a child is misbehaving, try to redirect or provide a distraction. For example, if a child wants another child's toy, offer that child some other options to play with. Sometimes distracting children by offering something completely different can cause them to take their mind off the initial object or situation that was stirring up frustration.

Children respond well to giving them two appropriate choices, either one of which would satisfy you. Let's say you really need a child to sit down. Say, "Do you want to sit in the blue chair or the red chair?" If he or she can't choose, then gently tell him or her that you'll have to choose. This is usually enough of a motivator for the child to make the choice on his or her own.

Your reaction to misbehavior is crucial. It can send many different messages. So stay calm and use a quiet, even voice. Refrain from making quick gestures, and kneel down to the child's level.

Many misbehaviors can be prevented by providing routine and structure. These provide security and predictability for toddlers, which foster better behavior patterns.

Most children respond very well to visual and auditory cues. To get children's attention you can use hand clapping and music. Using "feeling" posters with different emotional expressions on faces can help provide feeling "faces" for toddlers who cannot verbally express their emotions.

Setting Up a Toddler Classroom

A room that appeals to toddlers will invite children to explore, play and investigate. Toddlers will be entertained with just about anything, but it's important to keep in mind a few overall qualities and values in establishing and maintaining a toddler classroom. These qualities are all equally important when you are considering the setup and maintenance of a toddler classroom.

A warm and inviting atmosphere
Safety and maintaining a healthy environment
Communication with parents
Materials appropriate for toddlers' skill level and development

Get into the Zone

When planning a learning environment for toddlers, think of zones. Each zone will serve a different purpose. Depending on the size and arrangement of the room you may not need all five zones listed here, or you may choose to make more zones.

QUIET ZONE. This zone may have a mattress, pillows and books, and allow children the opportunity to rest, sleep or engage in quiet activities.

CHANGING ZONE. This zone is where diapers can be changed. Hopefully there is a sink available or the ability to sanitize the area after each use.

TABLETOP ZONE. This zone should have tables and chairs available to the children. Several different types of activities can occur here, such as art, snack or Bible memory.

OPEN SPACE ZONE. This area is where motor skills activities, construction activities and some games can be safely played.

STORY TIME ZONE. This area might also be marked with spots for the children to sit or a special colored rug. It can also be used as the dramatic play area.

Many toddler rooms appeal to adults, but are overstimulating for toddlers to handle. Too much of anything—toys, colors and noise—is not always a good thing for little ones.

Health and Safety Checks

Every toddler room should be checked before and after every use. Be sure to disinfect tabletops, countertops, doorknobs and toys on a regular basis. Check plugs, cords, screens, plants and other items that present dangers to children. Keep toys in good repair and use a choke tube to be sure that all toys will not be choking hazards. Anything that fits in a choke tube is too small to be in a toddler classroom. Be sure to post all local emergency contact numbers and clear steps for infant and toddler CPR.

Warm Relationships

With a room that is safe and appropriate for the little ones in your care, parents will feel better about leaving the children in the toddler room. Teachers will feel more comfortable with their responsibility to care for the children. Everyone will be able to focus on providing warm, caring and fun interactions with the children—and will leave a lasting impact on their faith development.

TODDLERS ON THE GROW
The Developing Mind

We are equipped with about 100 billion brain cells when we enter the world. We don't gain more brain cells as we grow, but we do develop pathways for how neurons transmit information. The most rapid development of connections and pathways in our brains occurs in the first three years of life. That means toddlers—the children you work with—are exploding with brain growth.

The Growing Brain

Here's what happens when toddler brains grow.

Imagination: The first year of life centers on developing physically and on gross motor skills. Toddlers are still refining gross motor skills but have slowed down their physical growth. They are now able to spend more energy developing more advanced cognitive skills. Toddlers enter into a new stage of brain development when they begin to use imagination and engage in pretend play. You will see them engage in imaginative and dramatic play through the experiences you provide for them.

Labels and symbols: Toddlers begin to understand labels for objects. Eventually, they develop the language to say what the object is. They love to look at pictures and point things out to you. Once they master the skill of identifying objects, they soon can attach meanings or symbols to objects. This becomes very important in faith development.

Follow directions and commands: Toddlers gain a better understanding of following simple one-step directions. Sometimes their understanding of directions and commands is much greater than we give them credit for. They will enjoy simple games as they learn to follow directions and commands.

The Growing Brain and Faith Development

Many concepts of faith are formed through the use of symbols and representations. When children understand that an object can represent or mean something else, they have discovered the basis of a symbol. They will be able to make connections between objects and concepts. A rainbow can mean "trust God." Enriched learning environments that encourage play also promote brain growth and connections. The more connections the brain makes with everyday objects in the context of faith, the more faith becomes intricately woven within the memory.

TODDLERS ON THE GROW
Social and Emotional Development

The toddler is an egocentric little person, and that's okay. That's what God planned. Being aware that the toddler's world is centered around "I" and "me" is especially important when you put several of them together in a classroom setting. Here is what's developing and happening in the typical toddler during this stage of social and emotional development.

IT'S MINE!: Most toddlers do have problems with sharing and cannot understand other points of view. When a child struggles with sharing, you can help by modeling how sharing would look. You can also use empathetic words to express emotions of how others might be feeling.

ALL BY MYSELF: At this stage of development toddlers like to play alone—unless, of course, another child has something they want. Eventually they will like to play alongside another child. Side-by-side play eventually will turn into social interactions.

RAGING RIVERS OF EMOTIONS: Toddler emotions seem to swing from one extreme to another. Tempers that flare usually are pent-up frustrations from the toddler's need for autonomy and inability to express needs and feelings. As toddlers increase their language and motor skills they will gain more control over their emotions.

MONKEY SEE, MONKEY DO: Toddlers love to imitate the actions of others, especially adults. If you show them what you want them to do, they will imitate you.

I DO IT!: Toddlers are beginning to show signs of independence. They can be quite demanding while trying to establish independence. This is because they have very little impulse control. They react to almost anything like a reflex. You'll often hear the words "No" and "I do." At this stage of development toddlers are trying out skills independently, and they want to do this without help. Give them many opportunities to do things on their own.

CUDDLE BUGS: As much as toddlers tend to have a lot of social and emotional struggles, most toddlers do love to be held and cuddled. They typically enjoy warm, loving adult interactions.

Emotional Growth and Developing Faith

A child develops trust on the platform of emotions. Children can love and trust someone to the degree of attachment they form. The social development of a child also plays an important role in developing skills of empathy. Experiences of empathy and tenderness lay the groundwork for understanding many concepts within faith development and the faith community.

TODDLERS ON THE GROW
Language Development

During the toddler stage of development, physical growth slows down some and language development takes off. The repertoire of words increases dramatically over a short period of time. Here are some other things to expect in the area of language development for the toddler.

COPY CATS: Toddlers will try out new words they hear or try to mimic words you say. They are able to repeat what you want them to say when prompted. This is a great time to surround children with language; as you're working, talk about what you're doing. Teaching new words to children can be exciting for both you and the child.

SONGS AND RHYMES: Children love to engage in singing simple songs and saying simple rhymes. The rhythms and sounds of music enhance language development and later reading skills. Experience the sounds of language together.

SENTENCES: Toddlers begin language development by expressing themselves with one or two words. As language develops, the number of words they put together increases. You can model using complete sentences by adding on to what the toddler says. Soon children learn that they can explain or defend themselves with words, they can ask for what they want, they can express their feelings and they can tell a story.

READING: Children love to listen to stories. They love to sit down with a book and "read." As a toddler gets older, you will begin to see that when they pick up a book on their own, they hold it the correct way. They will begin to point out things they notice in the illustrations. Reading opens up a whole new world of words and sounds to toddlers. Read to your children and make it as interactive as possible for this will make reading even more enjoyable.

Language Growth and Developing Faith

Language is the entry point to hearing and learning about God's Word. Show children the Bible. Point to the words you're reading from the Bible. Make reading something fun and exciting to experience. Stories are key to understanding the lessons God wants us to learn. In the Bible, God repeatedly teaches us through the use of story. Language opens the way for communication with God and about God. Children can experience God through stories, song, praying and talking to others.

PREPARE TO TEACH MORE TODDLERIFIC!

Each lesson in *More Toddlerific!* will equip you with ideas, activities and the faith concepts to engage children in directed play for 12 lessons. Each lesson falls under one of three themes, "All about God," "All about God and Me," and "All about God, Me and Others." Each lesson includes a Bible story, a Bible truth, a Bible memory verse, a Godprint, and 12 activities to choose from. The Godprint tells you what faith quality the lesson helps develop in children, based on toddler developmental needs. Spend as long as you wish on each lesson. You might choose to spend several weeks on the same lesson, repeating favorite activities and gradually introducing new ones.

So How Do I "Teach" Toddlers?

Toddlers learn as they are engaged through play. To teach toddlers you simply provide activities that keep them occupied and focused on play. Toddlers usually play alone or alongside each other. We understand that toddlers are not groupies. Getting toddlers together for a group lesson can be challenging and frustrating. Every Bible story and activity is designed to give you the flexibility in determining what works best for you. So every activity can be prepared for either small groups, large groups or for individual children.

How Do I Decide What to Do?

Just take your time and keep it simple. Each activity takes into account the short attention spans, interests and skill levels of toddlers. A reproducible page for each lesson will provide you with a hands-on presentation of the Bible story. Each of the 12 activities falls into one of the following categories: motor skills, art, snack, sensory exploration, dramatic play, preschool skill, construction, songs, rhyme time, game, tell-it-again and Bible memory. There is no particular order or sequence of the activities, so pick and choose whatever you wish. Remember, toddlers love repetition. You can use the same activities several weeks in a row, perhaps introducing one or two new ones each week.

How Do I Prepare It All?

Many of the materials needed for the activities can be found around the house, at a local discount store or stocked at the church. Once you have gathered the supplies you need, you are ready to put the activities together. A simple method of organizing and making activities easily accessible for you and others who might be helping you is to organize activities into zip-top bags. Place all the items needed to accomplish the activity in a large bag. Use a permanent marker to label the bag. Zip-top bags work well because they are so mobile. You can move from place to place with the child if you need to. It also makes for easy storage and accessibility.

"At Home in the Faith" and "What I Did Today" Reproducibles

At the end of each lesson is a parent reproducible called "At Home in the Faith." This helps to educate parents on concepts taught in your class. It also provides parents with faith-building activities for the home. If you choose to spread a lesson out over more than one week, you'll want to send this home just once.

Another parent reproducible, "What I Did Today" appears on page 111. Fill out this form every week to let parents know what their children did in class. Both handouts help parents in their important role in developing faith in children.

Child's name: _____

Today's Date: _____

What I Did Today

Your child had a wonderful time with More Toddlerific! Bible stories and activities. Here's what we did today.

Dear Mom and Dad,
This is what I learned today:

Bible Story: _____

Bible Truth: _____

Comments: _____

Teacher's Signature: _____

More Toddlerific! Copyright © David C. Cook. Permission to reproduce for local church use.

Baby Jesus

All about God: Knowing God includes knowing who he is and how he came to earth as baby Jesus.

Toddlers filled with Christmastime anticipation will be thrilled as you unwrap one of the most exciting gifts of all, the story of baby Jesus.

Toddlers are fascinated with babies. Build on this natural curiosity and introduce children to baby Jesus. Jehovah God came to us wrapped in a tiny little bundle of joy. Everyone was waiting with great anticipation for the time of the special delivery. Even men from far distances followed a star to find and worship the newborn King. You will have the opportunity to lay a foundation upon which the children in your care will be introduced to their King. Prepare the way for the King of all kings!

Through these activities, toddlers will learn about who God is, as Jesus the baby King. They will learn that Jesus was born and a special star in the sky led people to the baby. They will learn and practice skills in worshipping Jesus, the natural response that people have when they encounter God, their King.

Bible Truth:
God sent baby Jesus.

Bible Verse:
Jesus was born.
(Matthew 2:1)

Bible Story:
Unwrapping Christmas.
(Matthew 2:1–12)

Godprint:
Worship

"At Home in the Faith" Parent Reproducible p. 22

Unwrapping Christmas

GET LIST:

Bible Story Pictures for Lesson 1

Colored pencils or markers

Scissors

Gift wrap

Tape

Four boxes with separate lids

Color the Bible Story Pictures and cut them apart. Wrap the boxes and the lids separately, so the paper doesn't have to be torn to open the box. The boxes can then be used over again to retell the story. Put one Bible Story Picture in each box and place the lid on top. You might wish to number the boxes indicating the order of the Bible Story Pictures.

Pass the first gift around to the children. As you pass the gift say the following rhyme: **A special gift for us to see, sent by God for you and me.** Open the box. Show the children the picture and read the story segment. Repeat for all the boxes.

Bible Story Pictures Lesson 1

Picture 1: Baby Jesus

God sent a gift to us. The gift was baby Jesus. Jesus was born in a town called Bethlehem.

Picture 2: A Star

God sent a gift to us. The gift was baby Jesus. The star was shining above baby Jesus.

Picture 3: A Crown

God sent a gift to us. The gift was baby Jesus. Jesus was special. Jesus was going to be a king. People followed the star to find Jesus, the newborn King.

Picture 4: Gifts

God sent a gift to us. The gift was baby Jesus. The people saw Jesus and they were happy. The people worshipped Jesus and gave him gifts.

Baby Jesus 1

Stepping Stars

GET LIST

Construction paper

Scissors

Cut out twelve 6-inch stars from the construction paper. Scatter the stars on the floor. Tell the children about how the people jumped for joy when they saw the star. The star told them the baby Jesus was born. Have the children jump from star to star. As they jump have them shout out, "Jump for joy, Jesus was born!" To continue to play, have the children pick up the stars and let them place the stars on the ground themselves.

A Special Gift

GET LIST:

Wrapping paper squares

Picture of baby Jesus

Scissors

Glue stick

Crayons

Cut wrapping paper squares into the shape of a plus sign. Make the center of the plus sign about three inches square. Make copies of the baby Jesus picture for each child. Cut out the pictures and have the children color them. Tell the children they're going to wrap a special gift. Their gift will remind them of the special gift God gave to us, baby Jesus.

When children are finished coloring, ask each child, **What gift did God give to us?** Have the children respond with, "baby Jesus." Then have the children glue the baby Jesus onto the wrapping paper. Fold the paper so it wraps like a gift. Have the children take their gifts home. Be sure to label the back of the gifts with the children's names.

Star Bites

GET LIST:

Slices of cheese

Slices of lunch meat

Slices of bread

Star-shaped cookie cutter

Paper plates

Remind the children that when Jesus was born a special star shone in the sky. The star reminds us that Jesus was born. Celebrate the birth of Jesus around the snack table as the children make star-shaped snacks. You can help the children make their snacks using the cookie cutter. Make star shapes out of the bread, cheese and meat. The children can stack their stars into little sandwiches. *Be aware of children who may have wheat or milk allergies.*

Star Light

GET LIST:
Two flashlights

You can interact with the children two ways in this activity. Call a child over to play with you. Lie on your backs together, looking up. Encourage the child to look at the ceiling and look for the star. The star reminds us that Jesus was born. Flash your "star" light on the ceiling. Then hand the other flashlight, turned on, to the child. Have the child try to shine his or her light on your star. Move your star light around on the ceiling. Encourage the child to "chase" your star with his or her light.

To play another way, use only one flashlight. Stand in the room and shine your "star" light on the floor a little distance away from the child. Have the child try to catch your star by jumping on the light. Move the light on the floor to different spots.

Worship Baby Jesus

GET LIST:
Baby dolls
Baby blankets
Various baby items

Young children find babies fascinating. Provide baby dolls and baby items for the children to play with. Have the children pretend the dolls are baby Jesus. Remind the children that Jesus was a special baby sent by God. Jesus is a special gift to all of us. Have the children wrap up the baby Jesus as if they are wrapping a special gift. Talk about ways that we can worship or show Jesus we love him. Encourage the children to sing a song to Jesus, bring gifts to him or bow down to him.

Big Gift, Small Gift

GET LIST:
One large gift box
One small gift box

Play a game that uses gift boxes to remind the children that Jesus is a gift from God to us. Place the large gift box on the floor on one side of the room. Place the small gift box on the floor on the opposite side of the room. Call out a command such as "hop," "jump," "skip" or "crawl." Then shout out, "to the large box (or small box)." The children then have to move toward the selected box. Shout out changes in the command just before the children reach the box. Or as children reach the box, shout out, "Jesus is God's gift." You can also use different words referring to the size of the boxes such as big and little, tall and short.

Gift Boxes

GET LIST:

Three or four small gift boxes in different sizes

Large box of packing peanuts

Masking tape

Children will empty and fill gift boxes, a developmental skill they enjoy. Encourage the children to keep the packing peanuts inside the large box. Place the smaller gift boxes inside the larger one. Have them empty and fill the smaller gift boxes with packing peanuts. As they play remind the children that people brought gifts to the baby Jesus to show Jesus they loved him. We can give gifts to Jesus too. Have the children shout, "We love Jesus," when they fill or empty a gift box.

Sparkle, Sparkle Little Star

GET LIST:

No supplies needed

Celebrate the birth of a baby king. Sing to the tune of "Twinkle, Twinkle, Little Star."

> **Sparkle, sparkle, little star.**
>
> **We will follow near and far.**
>
> **Lead us to the baby king.**
>
> **We will praise him and we'll sing.**
>
> **Sparkle, sparkle, little star.**
>
> **We will follow near and far.**

Way Up High

GET LIST:

No supplies needed

Gather two or three children to sit with you. Say the poem several times. Then add some motions to the poem. Have the children join you as you repeat the phrase and motions.

Way up high in the sky

(Look up to the sky.)

There was a star shining bright.

(Make a star with your hands above your head, bringing your thumbs and index fingers together. Have the rest of your fingers spread apart.)

A baby boy who brings us joy

(Pretend to rock a baby in your arms.)

Was born to us that holy night.

(Point to yourself or the children for "us," then place hands folded as if sleeping for "night.")

Follow the Star

GET LIST:

Two-foot piece of streamer

Construction paper

Empty paper towel tube

Scissors

Tape

Cut out a large star from construction paper. Tape the star to one end of the streamer. Tape the other end of the streamer to the empty paper towel tube. Hold the tube up so that the star dangles for everyone to see. Gather the children to play a little game of follow the star. Remind the children that following the star led people to see the baby Jesus. As you lead the children around the room have them chant, "Follow the star." Give the children the opportunity to be the leaders.

Jesus Is Born

GET LIST:

Gift boxes from the Bible story

CD player

Christmas music CD

Tell the Bible story again. Hand the Bible story boxes out to the children. As the Christmas music plays have the children pass the gifts around to each other. When the music stops, open the first Bible story gift. Read the Bible Story Picture in the gift box. Remove the first Bible story gift from being passed. Start the music and pass the remaining gifts. Stop the music and open the second box. Read the Bible Story Picture in the gift box. Continue until all the gifts have been opened.

Jesus Is Born. (Matthew 2:1)

GET LIST:

Bible

Gather the children. Hold the Bible up for the children to see. Tell them, **This is God's book. God's book tells us Jesus was born.** Ask the children, **What does God's book tell us?** Have them respond with, "Jesus was born." Then say it again; this time, have children complete your sentence. Say, **God's book tells us....** Then have them complete your statement with, "Jesus was born." Continue to make statements children have to complete with, "Jesus was born." Some examples: **In the Bible it tells us ...., God sent a gift and ...., The star in the sky tells us that ...., The wise men knew that ...., People brought gifts because ...., We worship because ....**

At Home in the Faith

BiBLE TRUTH: God sent baby Jesus.

BiBLE VERSE: Jesus was born. (Matthew 2:1)

BiBLE STORY: Unwrapping Christmas. (Matthew 2:1–12)

GODPRINT: Worship

'Tis the season for...friends, family, food, fun—and Christ? Sometimes we get so wrapped up in the hustle and the bustle of the holidays we forget about the reason for the season. At the end of these busy days, set aside a little time every night as a family to focus on the birth of Jesus, our King and Savior. Read a story, sing a song or do an activity. Keep Christ the center of this joyous season.

Establishing Traditions

The Christmas season lends itself to establishing and continuing family traditions. Traditions leave a lasting impression on your child's life that will carry into adulthood. You can start traditions that are rich in keeping Christ and the biblical stories as the focus.

Here are a few suggestions based on the Bible story that your child learned in class. The story is found in Matthew 2:1–12. These are sure to put the spark of Christ into your Christmas celebrations.

· It's so hard to wait! Have your child open three little gifts the night before Christmas. The three gifts represent the three gifts the wise men gave to Jesus. Or, as a family, come up with three gifts that you can give to Jesus for the year.

· Every night light a candle representing the wondrous star that shone in the night, the star that guided the wise men to the location of Jesus. The star that told everyone that Jesus, the newborn King, the long-awaited Savior, had been born.

· Everyone was filled with joy at the news that the Savior had been born. As a family, brainstorm a list of things that bring you joy. Write down your ideas on pieces of wrapping paper. Tape the little messages of joy all around the house.

Placemats of Love

Make gifts for family and loved ones that leave a lasting impression. Purchase plain cloth placemats and iron-on transfer crayons. Have your child use the special crayons to draw on plain white copy paper. Drawings might include pictures, doodles and traced hands. Place the drawing crayon side down onto a placemat. Use an iron to transfer the drawing onto the placemat. Wrap the placemats and give as gifts to loved ones.

Christmas is a time to worship the birth of our King. Worship comes in many forms. One form loved by toddlers of all ages is music. Fill your house with Christmas music. Find time to dance, sing and worship the King!

Jesus Lives

All About God: Knowing God means learning he has the power over death, and to know his Son, Jesus, lives to give us eternal life.

Jesus lives! Jesus lives today! From death to life is a big concept for little ones, but everlasting love is not.

During Easter time most children will be hopping with excitement over visiting the Easter bunny, wearing new clothes, decorating eggs and filling Easter baskets. Strengthen the reason for the season by engaging your little ones in even more exciting news. Jesus is alive! Jesus died, but rose again and is alive and well today because he is God's Son. The resurrection is one of the foundational beliefs of the Christian faith. Although the death and resurrection of Jesus are hard concepts to understand, there lies within these concepts a simple yet powerful message: God's love for us. This message lays a foundation for knowing God that even toddlers can receive and understand.

Through these activities your little ones will learn to praise God and celebrate because Jesus died and rose again. They'll learn the stone was rolled away and the tomb was empty. He has risen indeed. Jesus lives!

Bible Truth:
Jesus died and rose again.

Bible Verse:
He is not here! He has risen.
(Matthew 28:6)

Bible Story:
The Stone Is Rolled Away. (Matthew 27:33—28:8)

Godprint:
Praise

"At Home in the Faith" Parent Reproducible p. 30

The Stone Is Rolled Away

GET LIST:

Bible Story Pictures for Lesson 2

Colored pencils or markers

Scissors

Brad

Color the illustrations for the Bible Story Pictures. Cut the pictures apart. Place the pictures in order and punch a hole where indicated. Insert a brad through the holes to make the Bible storybook. To begin the Bible story, align all the pictures behind #1, the Bible.

Bible Story:

· Start the story by turning to picture 6 and read it to the children.

Jesus died on the cross.

· Turn pictures 4 and 5 together so that only picture 4 shows. Read.

Jesus was buried in a tomb.

· Turn pictures 2 and 3 together so that only picture 2 shows. Read.

They rolled a stone in front of the tomb. Three days later the earth shook. Shake the pictures. **Then God rolled the stone away.**

· Now show picture 3. Read.

The angel said, "Jesus is not here. Jesus has risen."

· Turn picture 3 and 4 together to show picture 5. Read.

Jesus lives!

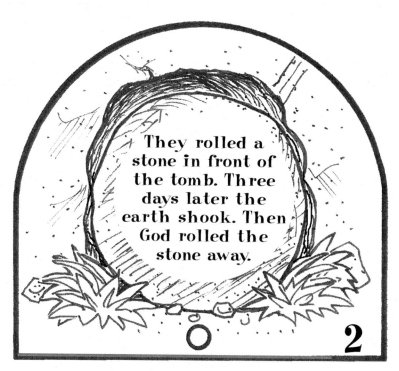

They rolled a stone in front of the tomb. Three days later the earth shook. Then God rolled the stone away.

The angel said, "Jesus is not here. Jesus has risen." **3**

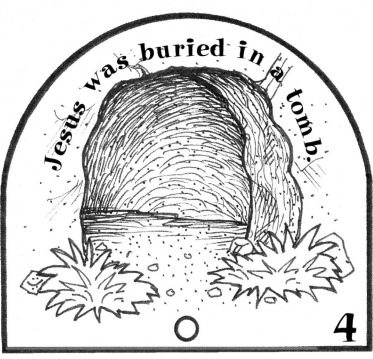

Jesus was buried in a tomb. **4**

5

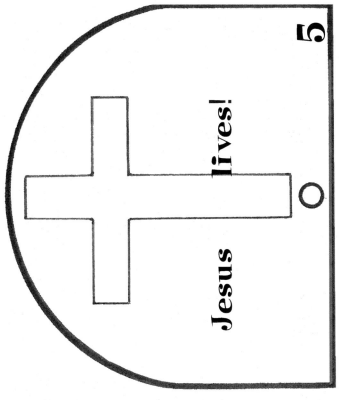

Jesus lives!

Jesus died on the cross. **6**

Rolling Stones!

GET LIST:

Large plastic kick ball

Large box

Scissors

Masking tape

Young children need lots of practice to develop their gross motor skills. This activity works on eye and foot coordination. One child at a time can play it over and over. Cut a very large arched opening on the side of the box. Make sure the opening is large enough for the ball to easily roll through it. The children will be trying to roll the "stone" (the ball) in front of the "tomb" (the box). Place the box on the floor. Use the masking tape to mark three different start lines. One line could be a short distance away from the box and the other two progressively further away from the box. Have the children take turns. As they roll the stone have them shout, "Roll the stone away." If the stone successfully enters the tomb, have the children shout, "Jesus lives!"

At the Cross

GET LIST

3 x 5 cards

Glue

Paintbrush

Chocolate puff breakfast cereal

Tape

Make a reminder for the children to take home that Jesus lives. This activity can be completed individually or in a small group. Cut the 3 x 5 cards into the shape of a cross. Make a cross for each child. Tape the crosses to the table. As the children approach, tell them that Jesus died on the cross. Then explain that Jesus didn't stay dead. The stone was rolled away and Jesus was not there. He's alive! Brush the crosses with glue. Have the children place the "stones" cereal onto the cross to remember that the stone was rolled away and Jesus lives!

Rolling Praise

GET LIST

Donut holes

Two or three pie tins

CD player

Children's praise music

The children will get rolling to some praise music as they snack on "stones." Invite two or three children to come to the snack table. Show the children the special "stones" you have for them (the donut holes). These stones will remind them that Jesus is alive and we're glad the stone was rolled away. Encourage children to praise God because Jesus is alive. As they listen to a song, challenge them to roll a "stone" in the pie tin for as long as the song plays. When the song is finished let them enjoy eating their "stones." *Be aware of children who may have food allergies.*

Crosses and Stones!

GET LIST

Play dough

Plastic or vinyl placemats

Encourage the children to use the play dough to make crosses and stones. As they work, tell them the cross reminds us that Jesus died. The stones remind us of when the stone was rolled away. Spread the excitement of knowing Jesus is alive. Have the children use the play dough on placemats for easy clean up. If you'd like to make your own dough, use this recipe.

Play dough

2 cups flour

1 cup salt

4 Tablespoons cream of tartar

2 cups warm water

2 Tablespoons cooking oil

Food coloring (several squirts)

Combine liquid ingredients in a saucepan and warm over medium heat. Stir together the dry ingredients in a separate bowl. Then add the dry ingredients to the contents of the saucepan. Stir thoroughly until a soft ball forms. Once cooled, store in zip-top bags.

Palm Branch Praise

GET LIST

Green streamers

CD player

Children's praise music

Use an area with some room to move to the music. Provide each child with one or two ribbons of streamers. Before the music begins, show the children how they can wave their "palm branches." Waving their palm branches is one way they can show God how happy they are that Jesus is alive. You might wish to encourage different types of movement during the music. Stop the music and say, **Now we will hop to the music as we wave our palm branches.** Use commands such as: skip, hop like a bunny, move backwards or jump up and down in place.

Roll Away

GET LIST:

Various size balls or items that will roll

Ramp (book, cookie sheet, box lids)

Hold the ramp by propping up one end and keeping the other end on the ground. Then have a child roll a ball down the ramp. The children will be very excited to see how far the ball rolls. Have the children experiment by using the different sized items to see which one will roll the farthest. Try rolling all the items again, this time changing the angle of the ramp. As children play, remind them the stone was rolled away because Jesus is alive!

Build a Cross

GET LIST:

Large craft sticks
Construction paper
Marker

This activity is a construction activity that does not require gluing, much like when a child builds with blocks. On the construction paper, draw a large basic shape of a cross. Have the children "build" with craft sticks. They can use the craft sticks by placing them onto the construction paper and filling in the shape of the cross. Tell them, **Jesus died on the cross, but the good news is that he rose again.** Once they are done filling in the cross have them shout, "Jesus lives!" or "Jesus rose again." They can clear the craft sticks off of their papers and begin again.

Where Is Jesus?

GET LIST:

No supplies needed

Hip-hip hooray, Jesus is alive today! Sing this cheerful song to the tune of "Where Is Thumbkin?"

Where is Jesus? Where is Jesus?

He has risen. He has risen.

The great big stone was rolled away.

Jesus is alive today.

Hip-hip, hooray.

Hip-hip, hooray.

Praise Cheers

GET LIST:

Pompoms or streamers

Cheering is one way that preschoolers can praise God. Here are two simple cheers that are sure to get the children chanting. Have the children use pompoms or streamers. You might wish to add actions to the cheers.

Rolling, rolling, roll the stone away.

Jesus is alive today, hip-hip hooray.

Singing, singing, sing a song of praise.

Jesus is alive and well, stand up and yell.

Rolling Stone Tag

GET LIST:

Large plastic kick ball

Sit in the center of the floor. Have the children gather around you. Explain that this is a game where the ball or "stone" is rolled away, just like they learned about how the stone was rolled away. When you say, "Roll the stone away," they can move anywhere in the room, but they don't want to get touched by the rolling "stone." Gently roll the ball at the children. It might take them a minute to get the hang of this. At first they might want to grab or kick at the ball. You might have to show them how to stay away from the ball. Once they understand, they'll shout out, "Roll the stone away" without any prompting because they want to play over and over again.

The Stone Is Rolled Away

GET LIST:

Bible Story Pictures (pages 24–25)

Gather the children. Take apart the Bible storybook. Spread the pictures on the floor. As you tell the Bible story, have the children help you select the picture that matches that part of the story. You can put the book back together as they select the pictures. When the book is completed once again, retell the story. Allow the children the opportunity to play with the Bible story booklet.

He is not here! He has risen. (Matthew 28:6)

GET LIST:

Bible
12–18 plastic eggs
Basket
Permanent marker

Hold up the Bible for the children to see. Tell them, **The Bible says Jesus is not here! He has risen.** On three of the plastic eggs, draw a small cross. Hold up one of the eggs with a cross on it for the children to see. Tell them that when they see this egg they are to say, "He is risen." Have the children practice. Then hold up a plain egg. When they see this egg, they say, "Jesus is not here." Have the children practice. Place all the eggs in the basket. Pull out an egg and have the children say: (if it is blank) "Jesus is not here" or (if it has a cross on it) "He is risen."

BiBLE TRUTH: Jesus died and rose again.

BiBLE VERSE: He is not here! He has risen. (Matthew 28:6)

BiBLE STORY: The Stone Is Rolled Away. (Matthew 27:33—28:8).

GODPRiNT: Praise

Great news! Jesus is alive! This news is one of the foundations of the Christian faith. As you pass on the good news message to your child through family activities and celebrations, you impact your child's developing faith. Although there is deep, reverent significance in the events that surround the death and resurrection of our Savior, there is also a joy and excitement that can hardly be contained. Share the joy that turned the world upside down with your child. Here are a couple suggestions in providing you the opportunity to turn your child's world right side up!

Easter Basket Praise

Take a familiar Easter item and turn it into an opportunity to teach your child about God. Easter is a time for celebration and praise, so teach your child how to praise God. Use plastic eggs in a basket. In each egg, place a slip of paper that states a way to praise God. Examples might include praying, singing, clapping, dancing and playing music. You could also write things on the papers that you praise God for. For example, "I praise God for Grandma, Mommy, flowers, Jesus," and so on. Throughout the day, ask your child to go to the "praise" basket and pull out an egg. Read the egg and together praise the Lord!

Easter Story?

Story time is very important in the development of the child. Make quality time to read to your child every day. During certain seasons and celebrations there are many exciting activities that children are engaged in that don't have any religious significance. So how does a toddler distinguish between the stories told about the "Easter Bunny" and the truths imparted to them about God's Son, Jesus? Well, they can't. But you sure can try to help them separate between the two different types of stories.

One way to distinguish the truth from "stories" is in the language we use. Refer to secular stories as "stories" and label Bible ones differently, such as "Bible truths" or say, "It's Bible truth time." Another way to separate the two is to always tell Bible "truths" in a consistent place such as a Bible time chair. Another way to help a child discriminate is to always show a real Bible before you read the illustrated or children's version of the Bible truth. Spread the good news, the truth!

Children function very well within structure and routines. Establish a daily routine that includes reading a book. A common nighttime routine might include the three Bs: bath, books and bed. Cherish the times you get to read together. It truly is a precious gift that can have effects that will forever impact your child's life.

God's Promises

All about God: To know God is to know the truths of his character. He never fails; he always prevails, so we can trust him, even when things seem grim. He always keeps his promises.

Who can anyone trust these days? Our world seems filled with empty and broken promises. Teach your little ones a valuable lesson: in God we trust!

The foundation of all relationships, present and future, is laid in the first three years of life. Relationships are built on the bedrock of trust. Toddlers seek to know whom they can trust. Help them embrace the one everyone can ultimately trust with their lives—God. When the storms of life come pouring down, show the children the way to God's ark of comfort and care. God is always there to protect us, guide us and to be with us. As children experience the sad realities of broken promises, be sure to point out the rainbow found in a God who always keeps his promises.

Through these activities the children will learn that God is the one to trust. God keeps his promises; he always has and always will.

Bible Truth:
God keeps his promises.

Bible Verse:
The Lord will keep all of his promises. (Psalm 145:13).

Bible Story:
Noah and the Ark. (Genesis 6:9—9:17)

Godprint: Trust

"At Home in the Faith" Parent Reproducible p. 38

Noah and the Ark

GET LIST:

Bible Story
Pictures for
Lesson 3

Colored pencils
or markers

Scissors

Color the illustrations and cut out the ark and rainbow figures. Fold on the lines indicated, so the figures can stand on their own.

1. Begin reading the Bible story by showing the children side 1 of the ark. Read: **There was a man named Noah. Noah was a good man. God told Noah to build an ark.**

2. Turn the ark to show side 2 and continue reading. **God told Noah to fill the ark with animals. God promised Noah he would protect him and the animals from a flood.**

3. Place the side of the rainbow labeled 3 so that it sits over the ark and read: **Then it rained and rained and rained! Noah and the animals were safe inside the ark, just as God had promised.**

4. Then turn the rainbow to show the side labeled 4. Read: **Then the rain stopped. The sun came out and God put a rainbow in the sky. God kept his promise to Noah. God always keeps his promises.**

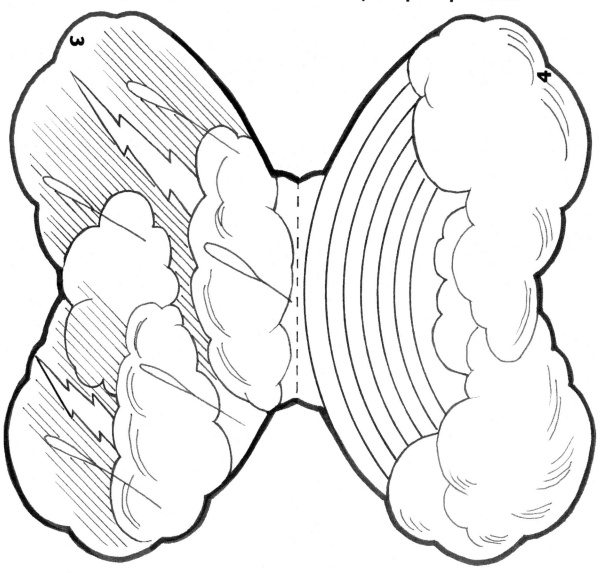

Rainbow Jumping

GET LIST:

Three or four swimming pool noodles in several colors

Lay the pool noodles on the floor side by side with about a foot of space between them. Tell the children, **This is a rainbow. The rainbow reminds you of how God keeps his promises.** Have the children form a line. To begin, have the children follow you. Lead them by walking or stepping over the rainbow strands. With each step, say one of the words in the phrase, **God ... keeps ... his ... promises.** After several attempts, move the strands either further apart or closer together. Allow time for the children to freely play with the rainbow.

A Rainbow of Promise

GET LIST:

Large sheets of white paper or butcher paper

Scissors

Markers

Tape

Cut the large sheet of paper into three or six strips that when put together will form a rainbow. Invite the children to come to the table. Everyone can help out by coloring a strip at a time with the same color. When one colored strip is completed, then bring out the next strip. Have the children color the second strip another color in the rainbow. The order of the colors of the rainbow are, from inside to the outside, red, orange, yellow, green, blue and purple. When the strips are completed, tape the rainbow together. Tell the children how the rainbow reminds you that God keeps his promises.

Banana Boats

GET LIST:

Bananas

Animal crackers

Plastic knife

Paper plates

Plastic bowl

Cut the bananas into three-inch chunks. Then take the chunks and hollow out a space in each one to form little boats. Place a boat on each plate. Put the animal crackers in a bowl. Let the children choose some animal crackers to put into their little boats. As the children enjoy their snacks, talk about how God told Noah to build a boat (ark). Tell them how God promised to keep Noah and the animals safe in his boat. Point out how their little boats can remind them to trust God because he keeps his promises. *Be aware of children who may have food allergies.*

A Rainbow of Colors

GET LIST:

Three different colored liquid dish soap

Zip-top bags that close tightly

White paper

Use the white paper as a mat for the children to work on. Call a child over to the table. Place the bag on the white piece of paper. Squirt a good amount, about one-third cup, of one of the dish soaps into the bag. Seal the bag and lay it flat on the mat. Let the child play with it by pressing down and drawing with his or her finger. Then open the bag and add a second color. Close the bag, place on the mat and give the child time to mix the colors. Then open the bag and add the third and final color. As children play, remind them that the colors in the rainbow remind us that God keeps his promises and we can trust him.

Noah's Boat

GET LIST:

Very large box
Stuffed animals
Scissors

Cut the box so that there is a door that can open and close. Leave the top of the box open or cut a large window on the top of the box. Tell the children they can pretend they are in Noah's boat (ark). God told Noah to build a boat (ark). Then God told Noah to bring the animals onto the ark. Add stuffed animals to the ark. God promised to keep Noah and the animals safe. God keeps his promises. Let the children play in the boat with the animals.

I See Rainbow Colors

GET LIST:

Construction paper sheets in red, orange, yellow, green, blue and purple

Let the children know that God put rainbows in the sky to remind us that he keeps his promises. **The rainbow is full of colors that are found around the room.** Have the children help you look for the colors of the rainbow in the room. Hold up a piece of red paper and say, **I see rainbow colors in the room.** Tell the children to look for something in the room that is red, matching the piece of paper you hold up. Repeat for all of the colors. When an item has been discovered, you might wish to take the paper to the item or have the child bring the item to you to match the colors. Not all the children know their colors by name, but they should be able to discriminate between the colors and match them with the one you are holding. If they don't match, be excited to find the colored sheet that does match, stating the correct color name.

Rainbow Links

GET LIST:

Yarn
Fruit-flavored cereal in circle shapes
Bowl
Tape
Scissors

The children will thread the fruit circle cereal onto a piece of string. Cut the yarn into 12-inch lengths. Fold a four-inch piece of tape in half on one end of each piece of yarn with the sticky sides together. This piece of tape will stop the fruit circles from falling off one end of the yarn. Show the children how to thread the yarn through cereal. For older children, you might wish to introduce using patterns with the different colors to make their rainbow links. As the children work, remind them that every time we see a rainbow in the sky it tells us God keeps his promises just like he did with Noah.

He's Got All the Animals in His Ark

GET LIST:

No supplies needed

Children will love to make up other lines to this song by using the animals they are familiar with. You might wish to include animal noises, motions and actions to this song. Sing to the tune of "He's Got the Whole World in His Hands."

He's got all the animals in Noah's ark. (Repeat two more times.)

God saves the whole world in Noah's ark.

He's got the silly little monkeys in Noah's ark. (Repeat two more times.)

God saves the whole world in Noah's ark.

He's got the happy hippos in Noah's ark. (Repeat two more times.)

God saves the whole world in Noah's ark.

He's got the tiny turtles in Noah's ark. (Repeat two more times.)

God saves the whole world in Noah's ark.

You can go on and on with any animal and a word to describe it.

Trust in God

GET LIST:

No supplies needed

This is a simple little rhyme. Invite one or two of the children over to where you are sitting. Start saying the rhyme. Say it several times. As you repeat the rhyme, start leaving out some of the rhyming words to see if the children can fill in the blanks for you.

God told Noah to build an ark.

He built the ark out of hickory bark.

He put the animals in the ark

Two by two just like a zoo.

Then it rained and poured a lot.

The ark, it was a nice safe spot.

What is this all teaching you?

Trust in God, he'll see you through.

God Key...ps His Promises!

GET LIST:

A key

Have the children sit in a circle. Have the children practice passing a key to each other around the circle. Then take the key and hold it up for the children to see. Tell them, **This key reminds you of the promises God key...ps. Every time you see a key you can remember God key...ps his promises.** Have the children pass the key around again, this time close your eyes. Wait a few seconds, then say, **Who key...ps his promises?** Then whoever has the key raises it in the air and shouts out, "God key...ps his promises." Repeat until everyone has had a turn.

Noah and the Ark

GET LIST:

Bible Story
Pictures for Lesson
3 (pages 32-33)

Hold the Bible story pictures behind your back. Walk around the room saying, **Noah, Noah and the _____.** To fill in the blank, hold up the Bible Story Picture of the ark. Have the children respond shouting the word, "ark." Then say, **Promises, promises, God keeps his promises, when I see a _____.** To fill in the blank, hold up the Bible Story Picture of the rainbow. Have the children respond shouting the word, "rainbow." Do this throughout your time together. After modeling this several times, you might wish to let a child help you hold up the correct pictures for the rest of the children to see.

The Lord Will Keep All of His Promises. (Psalm 145:13)

GET LIST:

Bible

God keeps his promises; this is something to cheer about. Hold up the Bible for the children to see. Tell them, **This is the Bible. The Bible has God's words in it. The Bible tells us the Lord will keep all of his promises.** Then ask like a cheer, **Who will keep all his promises?** Have the children shout the response, "The Lord will keep all his promises." Repeat this several times. You might wish to interject different questions such as, **Who keeps his promises to Noah?** Or **Who keeps his promises to you?** Or **Who always keeps his promises?**

BIBLE TRUTH: God keeps his promises.

BIBLE VERSE: The Lord will keep all of his promises. (Psalm 145:13)

BIBLE STORY: Noah and the Ark. (Genesis 6:9—9:17)

GODPRINT: Trust

The Bible is filled with illustrations of how God is trustworthy. The story of Noah and the ark is a wonderful example of how we can trust God. Trusting God allows us to weather the tough times. It allows us to rest in God's understanding and not our own. When children trust, it's like floating in the ark. They are free to grow and develop in the safety and care of the ultimate captain, God. You can show your children how deeply you trust the captain of your life, just as Noah did.

ALL ABOARD!

God is the captain of the ark in your house. Have a great time with your child as you pretend to play, "Noah and the Ark." This works great if you have a sofa-bed. Pull the bed out and pretend it's your ark or boat. An air mattress or blanket can make a great ark too. Then gather the animals from around your home, from stuffed to real ones. Have a rockin' good time together on the ark. Talk about how God promised Noah he would be with him. Noah trusted God to keep him and the animals safe from the wind, the rain and the wild water. Talk about times you have trusted God. When you're finished playing, your child will know that you would jump into any boat with God because he always keeps his promises.

PROMISES FROM THE HEART

Parenting is a joy, but sometimes life gets a little overwhelming and we need some help focusing on the little things. The little things we do—or forget to do—really build or damage the human element of trust. God has entrusted your child to you. He trusts you to love and care for your little one as he would. Here's a little activity that helps you focus on your child. Cut out four hearts from construction paper. Think about the things that your child likes to do—paint her nails, play hide and seek, have his back scratched, bake cookies, and so on. Write one activity on each heart. Attach the hearts to the refrigerator within the reach of your child. These are your promises to care and love your little one. Have your child randomly select a heart throughout the week. Enjoy the activity with your child as you lay the foundation of a trusting relationship.

The trust relationship you have with your child is the foundation upon which he or she will build trust in God.

Jesus Is Powerful

All about God: To know God is to know that he holds the ultimate power of the universe in the palm of his hand—the same hand he stretches out to reach for us.

To toddlers, everyone is a superhero. Introduce them to the most powerful superhero of all, Jesus.

Nothing wows a toddler more than a superhero. Of course, a superhero to them is anyone who is taller and able to do the things they can't do for themselves. Wow your little ones as you teach them about Jesus, the Son of God, who does extraordinary things. He is all-powerful and almighty. But best of all, Jesus, the superhero of the universe, wants to be their best friend. He wants them to know he has the power to do anything.

Through these activities, the children will learn that Jesus is powerful and mighty. They will learn about how amazing Jesus is because he can do extraordinary things.

Bible Truth:
Jesus has power.

Bible Verse:
His power is mighty.
(Psalm 147:5)

Bible Story:
Jesus Calms the Storm.
(Mark 4:35–41)

Godprint:
Awe and Wonder

"At Home in the Faith"
Parent Reproducible
p. 46

Jesus Calms the Storm

GET LIST:

Bible Story Pictures for Lesson 4 copied on cardstock

Colored pencils or markers

Scissors

Color the illustrations on the Bible story strip and cut it out. Color and cut out the boat. Cut the lines indicated on the boat. Slide the story strip through the top slit on the boat and thread it down through the bottom slit. Start the story at the first picture, then pull the story strip down to reveal the next picture in the Bible story. Read the story segment that appears beside each picture on the strip.

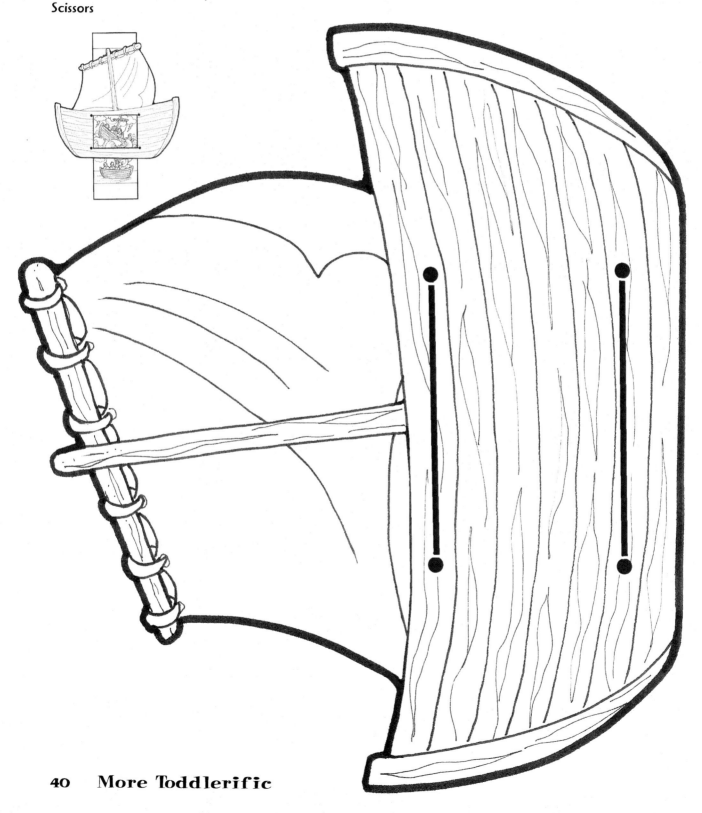

Bible Story Pictures Lesson 4

Picture 1

Jesus and some friends were on a boat.

Picture 2

A storm started to blow. The waves were big. The boat began to rock.

Picture 3

The friends were afraid. They called out to Jesus.

Picture 4

Jesus told the wind and the waves to stop, and they did. The waves stopped and the wind stopped. Jesus is powerful!

Bouncing Boats

GET LIST:

Four or more hula hoops

Masking tape

Children will enjoy bouncing from boat to boat as they cross the lake. Use the tape to mark off the boundaries of a large six- to ten-foot square on the floor. This is the lake. Lay the hula hoops inside the square. The hoops are the boats. The challenge for the children is to cross the lake without stepping into the water. Show them how they will have to step into the boats to cross the lake. Make sure the hula hoops are close enough together so the children can step from one hoop to the next. To make the activity more challenging spread the hoops out or remove one. As the children bounce from one boat to another, remind them of the events in the Bible story. Tell them how Jesus and his disciples were on a boat crossing a lake.

Stormy Boats

GET LIST:

Construction Paper

Card stock

Scissors

Screen or metal strainer

Toothbrush

Tempera paint

Small paper cups

Box lid

Tape

Cut a simple boat shape out of the card stock. This boat will be used as a pattern over and over again. Pour a little bit of the tempera paint into a cup. Tape a piece of construction paper to the inside of the box top. Place the boat pattern over the top of the paper. You might need a little bit of tape on the back of the boat to keep it in place. Call a child over to the table. Hold the screen or the strainer over the paper in the box top. Dip the toothbrush into the paint. Help the child create a storm by raining paint—brushing the paint—over the screen onto the paper. Once the "storm" has stopped, remove the boat from the paper. As you work with the child, talk about how Jesus has power to stop storms.

Peachy Boats

GET LIST:

Peach halves

Graham cracker bears

Paper plates with rims

Spoons

Place a peach half on each plate. Tell the children this is a boat. Hand out several graham cracker bears to each child. Have children put the "little people" into the boats. Remind them of how Jesus and his friends (disciples) were in a boat crossing a lake, when all of a sudden, a storm began to blow. Show the children how to gently tip their plates to move the "boat" around the plate. **Jesus' friends were scared.** Have the children make scared faces. **Then, Jesus told the storm to stop.** Have the children set their plates down. Tell the children, **Jesus is very powerful; he can make storms stop.** Let the children enjoy eating their boats. *Be aware of children who may have food allergies.*

Stormy Sea

GET LIST:

Clear plastic jars with lids
Vegetable oil
Blue food coloring
Glitter

Children will be able to create a stormy sea in a jar. Fill the jars two-thirds full of water and add only one drop of food coloring. Add one-fourth cup vegetable oil. Add a pinch of glitter. Tightly close the lids. Talk about how Jesus was in a boat with the disciples when a storm started to blow. Show the children how to swirl the water around, creating a "storm" inside the jar. Explain how Jesus' friends were afraid of the storm, so Jesus told the storm to stop. Set the jar down. Instantly the storm stopped. Jesus has the power to stop storms. Jesus has the power to do anything. Let the children explore with the jars.

Boat Ride

GET LIST:

Large box
Scissors

Cut the box top off. Tell the children this is a boat. Have the children act out the story as you explain how Jesus and the disciples used a boat to cross the sea. **When they were on the boat, a great big storm started to blow.** Have the children wave their arms and howl like the wind. **The boat started to rock from the high waves.** Have the children rock. **The men in the boat were afraid.** Have the children show scared faces. **Jesus saw that his friends were afraid. Jesus stood up and told the storm to stop**. Have the children stand and put out their hands showing "stop." **The storm stopped. The friends were amazed.** Have the children show what amazed faces look like. **Jesus stopped the storm. Jesus has the power to stop the storm. Jesus is powerful.** Have the children cheer. When you are finished, allow time for children to freely play in the boat.

Blowing Boats

GET LIST:

Large foam cups
Tub full of water
Scissors
Permanent markers

Cut the foam cups so that only one-fourth of the cup remains. These will be the little boats. To distinguish one boat from another you might wish to use markers to give each boat a splash of color. Or if the children will be able to take a boat home, label it with the child's name. Place the boats in the tub of water. As children approach the designated area, assign each one a boat. Have them produce a storm by blowing their "boats" (cups) across the water from one side of the tub to the other. As the children play, remind them of the Bible story. Tell them how Jesus had the power to stop a storm. Jesus has the power to do anything.

Building Boats

GET LIST:
Blocks
Picture of boats

Provide pictures of different boats from modern and Bible-time boats. Encourage the children to use the blocks to build one of the boats from the selection of pictures provided. When the children have completed their boats, see if you can guess which boat each one has copied. Remind the children that in the Bible story, Jesus' friends were on a boat with Jesus. When the storm came the boat began to rock and the friends were afraid. So Jesus stopped the storm because he is powerful. Jesus has the power to do anything.

Jesus Calms the Mighty Storm

GET LIST:
No supplies needed

Sing this song to the tune of, "Here We Go 'Round the Mulberry Bush." You can get this song a rockin' and a rollin' with some simple hand and body motions.

Here we go fishing in our boat, in our boat, in our boat.

Here we go fishing in our boat, on a calm blue sea.

The thunder clouds come rolling in, rolling in, rolling in.

The thunder clouds come rolling in. It's a stormy sea.

Jesus calms the mighty storm, mighty storm, mighty storm.

Jesus calms the mighty storm. It's now a calm blue sea.

Mighty God

GET LIST:
No supplies needed

Gather the children together. Use this simple rhyme to teach the children that the mighty God of the universe loves them too! Repeat the rhyme several times. Then have the children join you.

Jesus is a mighty God, a mighty God is he.

He stops the storm and calms the sea,

The mighty God loves me.

Stop the Storm

GET LIST:

Large playing area

Have all the children start at one end of the playing area. You stand at the other end. Tell them that when you say, **Stormy sea**, they can start to come towards you. When you shout, **Stop the storm**, they must freeze. Have the children practice until they understand the command. Start the game by calling out commands until all of the children reach you. After playing, remind the children how Jesus has the power to stop storms. Jesus has the power to do anything.

Jesus Calms the Storm

GET LIST:

Bible Story Pictures for Lesson 4 (pages 40-41)

Children enjoy hearing the Bible story over and over again. As children are engaged in play, go to them and ask if they would like to hear the story again. When they say yes, demonstrate how the Bible story strip works as you retell the Bible story. Then hand the Bible story boat to the child. Ask the child to pull the story strip as you tell the Bible story again.

His power is mighty. (Psalm 147:5)

GET LIST:

Bible
Child's size shirt
Newspaper or tissue paper

What is mighty power to a toddler? Big muscles! Invite a child to your area. Hold up the Bible. Tell the child that in the Bible it says, his power is mighty. Put the shirt on the child. Stuff the paper into the sleeves to look like muscles. Ask the child, **Whose power is mighty?** Have the child respond by bending arms up like flexing muscles and pointing heavenward. Then say, **His power is mighty.** Repeat several times. Remind each child the Bible tells us Jesus is the one with mighty power.

BiBLe TRUTH: Jesus has power.

BiBLe VeRSe: His power is mighty. (Psalm 147:5)

BiBLe STORY: Jesus Calms the Storm. (Mark 4:35–41)

GODPRiNT: Awe and Wonder

Today your child learned about the power of God. Jesus is so powerful and mighty that he can stop the wind and the waves. He can stop a storm. Even though your little one will not understand the implications of a God who is all-powerful, he or she will be in awe over the extraordinary display of his power. Your child will understand that Jesus is different from an ordinary person. Wow, your child with knowing Jesus, the all-powerful and mighty God, who is a welcomed guest in your house.

JeSUS COLLAGe

Introduce your child to the amazing, the wonderful and the powerful Jesus. Make a collage. Find different pictures of Jesus in magazines and coloring books. Cut them out and put them on a pasteboard or poster board. Talk about all the amazing things Jesus has done. You might wish to add pictures of other extraordinary things that Jesus has done from various different Bible stories. Then throughout your day, whenever a superhero is needed, go to Jesus.

STORM iN a BOTTLe

Make a storm in a bottle. Fill a clear jar three-fourths full of water. Add one drop of blue food coloring. Then pour in one-fourth cup vegetable oil. You might even wish to put in a pinch of glitter. Cap it tightly. Then hold the bottle. You can rock the bottle back and forth to make waves. Or you can swirl the bottle around in the same direction creating a mini tornado effect. Talk about how Jesus has the power to stop a storm. Then together you can praise Jesus for his amazing power.

Just think: if your child is amazed by you and your sheer size, think how God will seem even more amazing to him or her. Wow, your child by talking about how amazing the powerful, wonderful, creator and almighty God is, has been and will be to you.

Lost and Found

All about God and Me: To know God is to know he intimately and personally loves me. Because God loves me, I am very valuable and precious. To God, there is nothing more important than me.

Gather the little lambs in your care and tell them how precious each one is to the great shepherd.

At this young age, toddlers are consumed with themselves. They definitely are in the "me" stage of their lives. This stage is important to their development. It may seem they have no problem with their self-concept, when in fact it is fragile at this stage. Toddlers need to know without a shadow of doubt that they are precious and highly valued by God. They need to know that if they are ever lost or have gone astray, God, the Good Shepherd, will never stop hunting for them.

Through these activities, toddlers will learn that they are highly valued and precious, and they are worth much.

Bible Truth:
I'm Important to Jesus.

Bible Verse:
You are worth much.
(Luke 12:24)

Bible Story:
The Lost Sheep Is Found. (Luke 15:3–7)

Godprint:
Preciousness

"At Home in the Faith" Parent Reproducible p. 54

The Lost Sheep Is Found

GET LIST:

Make a copy of the Bible Story Pictures sheep mask for each child

Make one copy of the Bible Story Pictures shepherd's staff

Colored pencils or markers

Scissors

Color the shepherd's staff and cut it out. Cut out the sheep masks and the center portion of each mask. The children will be holding the masks up to their faces as you read the Bible story. Tell the children they will be helping you tell the Bible story. Whenever you see the shepherd's staff, point to the children and have them baa like sheep. Practice pointing and "baaing" before telling the story.

This story is about a shepherd and little sheep. I am the shepherd and you are the sheep. The shepherd watches over the little sheep. The shepherd loves his sheep. The shepherd sees one of his sheep is missing. A little sheep is lost. The shepherd looks high. The shepherd looks low. The shepherd looks everywhere for the little lost sheep. The shepherd finds the precious little sheep. The little sheep and the shepherd are very happy. Jesus wants you to know you are precious like the little sheep.

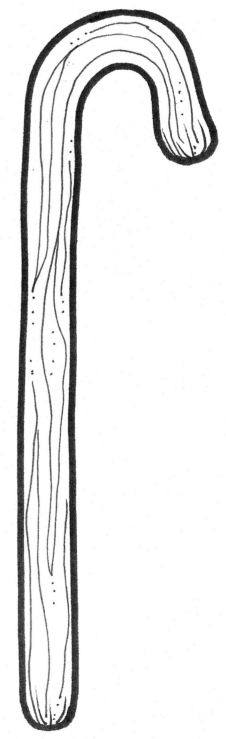

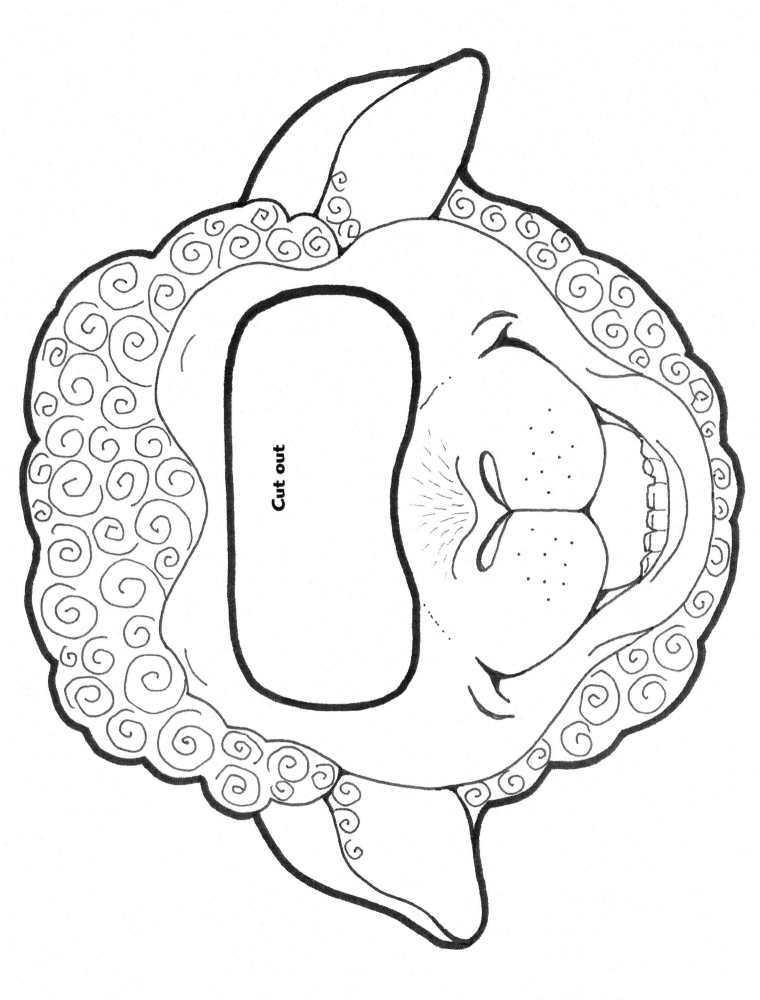

Cut out

Pick-Up Lost Sheep

GET LIST:

Cotton balls

Small brown paper bags

Spread out the cotton balls on the floor. Tell the children they are shepherds and that all shepherds have sheep. Point to the cotton balls and tell the children these are some lost sheep. As shepherds, they don't want any of their sheep to be lost. Every sheep is loved and is precious. Have the children pick up the lost sheep and put them into their bags. Remind them how Jesus loves them and how valuable they are to him. They are important to Jesus just like sheep are important to the shepherd.

I'm Precious

GET LIST:

Cotton balls

Construction paper

Scissors

Glue

Foil

Cereal bowl

Pencil

Turn the cereal bowl upside down on the foil. Trace around the bowl and cut out the circle. Glue the foil circle, shiny side up, onto a piece of construction paper. Above the circle, write, "I'm precious." Make one for each child. As the children approach the table, help them glue cotton balls around the foil. Talk about how the cotton balls remind you of little sheep and how Jesus loves his sheep. When they are finished, say, **Who is precious?** Have the children look into the foil. Then say, _____ (use his or her name) **is precious.**

Sweet Little Lambs

GET LIST:

Pears

Spoons

Whipped cream in a can

Paper plates

Chocolate chips

Place pear halves round side up and cut side down. Cover the pear halves with the whipped cream. Place two chocolate chips in the whipped cream for little eyes. Have the children "baa" like sheep. Say to them, **Oh, little lambs, little lambs, where are you little lambs?** Have the children continue to "baa." Point to the sweet little lamb snacks. **I see a sweet little lamb.** Let the children eat their lambs. Tell them how much Jesus loves them, just like a shepherd loves each of his sweet little lambs. *Be aware of children who may have food allergies.*

A Sheep's Touch

GET LIST:

Large sheet of construction paper

Glue

Swatches of different types of cloth

Sandpaper

Wrapping paper

Foil

Cotton balls

Scissors

Markers

You might wish to prepare this before class, or you could have the children help you make it. On the construction paper, draw the outline shape of a sheep as large as possible. Cut all of the tactile items you have gathered into squares. Glue the squares inside the outline of the sheep. For the cotton balls, glue a clump of them on paper in the shape of a square. Have the children explore all of the different textures of the items on the sheep. Tell them the sheep reminds you of how Jesus loves them. Tell them how important they are to Jesus, just like each sheep is important to the shepherd.

All about Me

GET LIST:

Assorted mirrors

Children love looking at themselves in the mirror and can learn so much about themselves from the experience. Allow them opportunity to explore with the mirrors. Then take some time to interact with them. As they play point out their physical characteristics. Say, **Look at your blue eyes!** Ask them to touch or point to their nose, eyes, hair, chin, cheek, tongue, ear, etc. Have them look **into the mirror and ask them questions such as, Who loves you? Who is important to Jesus (God)? Who is loved by Jesus (God)? Who is worth much? Who is special?**

Counting Sheep

GET LIST:

Egg cartons

Index cards

Scissors

Markers

Copy of Circle Sheep (below)

Cut the top off of the egg carton and discard. Use the part of the carton where the eggs sit. Use the markers to label the bottom of each egg holder with a number from 1 to 12. Cut 12 tiny little sheep (below). Call your little lambs over to the table. Have the children play by placing one sheep into each egg holder. Then they dump them out and start all over again. One-to-one correspondence is a very important developmental math skill. For older toddlers you might wish to help them count the sheep as they play.

Building Sheep

GET LIST:

Large and small marshmallows

Bowl

Placemats

Pretzel sticks

Wipes

Have the children pretend that the marshmallows are sheep. Give each child a placemat to work on. They can play with the sheep and use the pretzel sticks lying down as outlines of fences. You can pretend that a sheep is lost and they can rescue the lost the sheep. As they play you can remind them that shepherds love and care for their sheep. Every sheep is important to the shepherd. Tell them how they are just like sheep to Jesus. He loves and cares for them and each and every one of them is important. Have wipes available for sticky fingers.

Baa, Baa Lost Sheep

GET LIST:

No supplies needed

Children can pretend to be sheep during this song. Sing this song to the tune of, "Baa, Baa Black Sheep." You'll only be repeating the first refrain of the tune. You might wish to add motions to this song.

Baa, baa, lost sheep, where did you go?

Looking, looking, to and fro.

Baa, baa, lost sheep, we love you so.

Looking, looking, to and fro.

Little Lamb

GET LIST:

Stuffed lamb

Place the stuffed lamb somewhere in the room. Say the poem to the children and ask them to help you look for the little lamb. Repeat the poem over and over until the children have found the lamb. Then have everyone give the lamb a great big hug.

Little lamb, little lamb, where can you be?

You are very precious, to Jesus and me.

Little lamb, little lamb, we sure love you.

You are worth a million, it is true.

Find the Lost Sheep

GET LIST:

Stuffed sheep

Before class hide a stuffed animal sheep somewhere in the classroom. Then tell the children, **Oh where, oh where has our lost sheep gone?** Let children know there is a lost sheep somewhere in the room and you need their help. Make an urgent plea for them to help you find the lost sheep. Tell them whenever they hear a "baaing" sound that means someone is close to finding the lost sheep. As a child approaches the place where the sheep is hidden, begin to "baa" loudly. When the sheep is found, have everyone shout, "The lost sheep is found!" To play again, have the children close their eyes and hide the sheep.

The Lost Sheep Is Found

GET LIST:

Bible Story
Picture sheep
mask (page 49)

Hide the Bible story sheep face behind your back. Visit individual children or small groups of two or three children. Ask them if they have seen any sheep in the room. Then pull out the Bible story sheep face. Ask if anyone wants to be the little lamb as you tell the Bible story. Interact with the child as if he or she is a little lamb. Direct the children and have them "baa" as you retell the Bible story. Give them time to play freely with the Bible story sheep.

You are worth much. (Luke 12:24)

GET LIST:

Bible
Pretend paper
money
Tape

Invite a child over to your area. Hold up the Bible. Tell the child that the Bible says that, **You** (point to the child) **are worth much.** Show the money to the child. Ask if he or she knows what this is. Tell them it is money. Money is very important and is worth much. Spread the money on the floor. Ask the child to pick up one of the dollar bills and bring it to you. Then tape the money to the child. As you tape it to him or her say, **You are worth much.** Repeat until all of the money as been taped on. Then ask the child, **What are you worth?** Both of you say together, **You are worth much.**

Bible Truth: I'm important to Jesus.

Bible Verse: You are worth much. (Luke 12:24)

Bible Story: The Lost Sheep Is Found. (Luke 15:3–7)

GodPrint: Preciousness

You have been given a most precious gift to cherish and treasure—your child. Show your child how much he or she is valued and cherished by you, and by Jesus, too. You can't even put a price on the value of one of God's little lambs; we are all priceless in the eyes of the great shepherd. Show your child how much value you place on him or her with these activities.

Special Blessing Day

In the hustle and bustle of everyday life, we rarely take time to celebrate the person our child has become and is becoming. A blessing is not only a stamp of approval, but it is a hope and wave of encouragement for the child to ride for the next year. It is a time for reflection and for picturing someone's future as well. Set aside a day, perhaps six months from your child's birthday, to celebrate as a special blessing day. This day should stand out and be celebrated a little differently than a birthday. Little ones will soon look forward to their "special blessing" day.

I'm Important

There will never be another child like yours. Pass on the message of how unique, valuable and important he or she is to you. Use a large piece of paper—perhaps white wrapping paper. Have your child lie down on the paper. Use a marker to trace around your child. Write your child's name on the drawing. Have your child help you color in the picture. As you work, talk about all the special characteristics your child has.

Every day, use positive words of praise and encouragement with your child. Post a list of phrases and words you can use on your refrigerator as reminders. There is power in the positive!

Talk to God

All about God and Me: To know God is to know he wants me to be in constant communication with him. I can go directly to God and tell him everything.

Talk, talk, talk—this is what toddlers love to do.

Toddlers have a natural bent for talking. They are learning every day new aspects of language and new words. Take this natural instinct and bend it in God's direction. Prayer is simply talking to God. You don't need to bow your head or fold your hands every time, though there are times for that. Teach your little ones to have daily conversations with God. Toddlers love to talk, even when people aren't there to listen. Let them know God is always there and he is continually listening.

Through these activities your toddlers will have numerous opportunities to talk to God. They will learn that God is always listening.

Bible Truth:
I can pray to God.

Bible Verse:
Tell God about everything.
(Philippians 4:6)

Bible Story:
Samuel Talks to God.
(1 Samuel 3:1–4:1)

Godprint:
Prayerfulness

"At Home in the Faith" Parent Reproducible p. 62

Samuel Talks to God

GET LIST:

Bible Story
Pictures for Lesson
6 on cardstock

Colored pencils
or markers

Tape

Small craft stick

Scissors

Small piece of
cloth

Color the bed and Samuel. Cut out the figures on the solid lines. On the bed, cut the solid lines on the bedposts up to the dots. Fold the legs back on the dotted lines. Fold the headboard up; this will make the legs point down. Fold the footboard down; this will make the other pair of legs point down. The bed should now be able to stand freely.

Fold the bottom part of Samuel back. Tape the bottom part of Samuel to the end of the bed. Cut a hole in the middle of the bed, where indicated. Insert the craft stick up through the bed and tape the stick to the back of Samuel. Be sure that as you push the stick back and forth, it appears that Samuel lies down and sits up in bed. Use the piece of cloth as a blanket to cover Samuel. As you tell the story, the blanket will most likely fall off when Samuel pops up. Every time Samuel lies down again, place the blanket over him. Show the children the bed with Samuel lying down and begin reading the Bible story.

There was a boy named Samuel. (Show Samuel popped up in the bed.)

He was tired and went to bed.
(Show Samuel lying in bed.)

One night when Samuel was sleeping, he heard someone calling his name. "Samuel, Samuel."

Samuel jumped up. (Pop Samuel up.)
But no one was there.

So Samuel went back to bed. (Show Samuel lying in bed.)

Then Samuel heard the voice again calling his name. "Samuel, Samuel." Samuel jumped up again. (Pop Samuel up.) **But no one was there.**

Samuel went back to bed. (Show Samuel lying in the bed.)

Tape to bed.

Samuel heard the voice again calling his name. "Samuel, Samuel." Samuel jumped up one more time. (Pop Samuel up.)

This time Samuel talked to God. Samuel learned to tell God everything.

You can talk to God day or night, because God is always listening. You can tell God everything, just like Samuel.

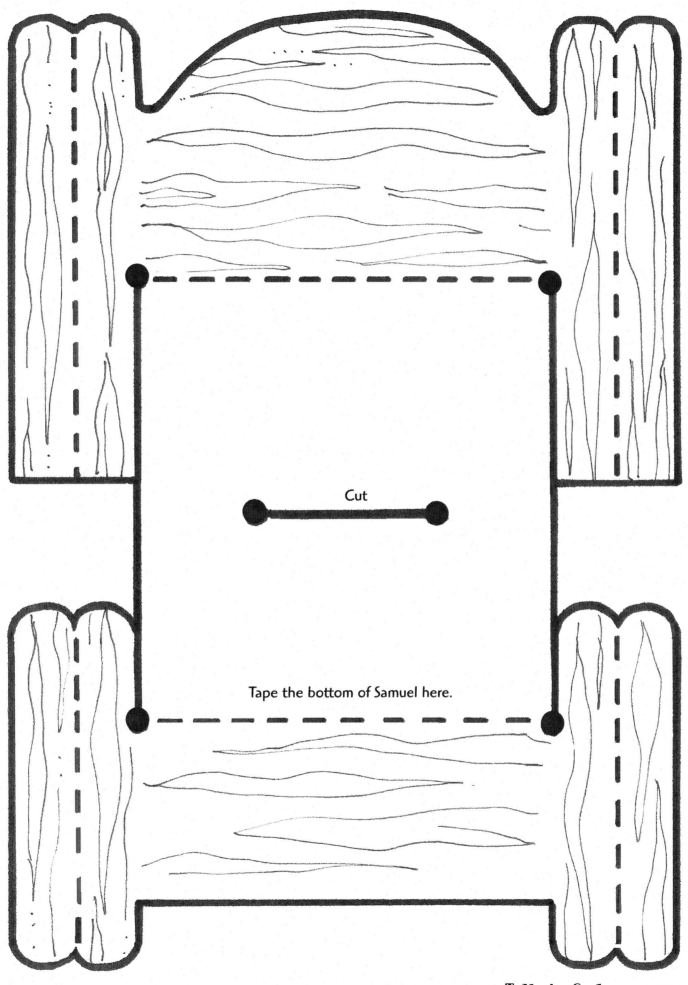

Cut

Tape the bottom of Samuel here.

Samuel's Blanket

GET LIST:

Large blanket
Balloon
Permanent marker

This is a group activity. Blow up the balloon and draw a smiley face on it. This is Samuel. Spread the blanket on the floor. Have the children sit around the blanket. Tell the children how the blanket reminds you of bedtime and how they learned about Samuel's bedtime story. Have the children grab onto the edges of the blanket. Introduce them to Samuel by placing the balloon in the center of the blanket. Have the children wave their arms up and down, causing the balloon to go into the air. As the balloon lifts up, have them shout out, "Samuel." When you are finished playing, do not leave the balloon unattended. Keep the balloon out of the reach of children when you are not using it.

Bedtime Blanket

GET LIST:

Copy paper
Fabric transfer
crayons
Iron
Old white bed
sheet or dish towel

Cut the copy paper into four equal squares. As the children approach your table, hand them a square. Have the children color the square. Encourage them to fill in as much of the square with color as possible. While they color, talk about the Bible story. Tell them how Samuel talked to God. Talk about things from the Bible story that they could draw. When they are finished, tell them you are going to use all their drawings to make a bedtime blanket. Turn the pictures with the crayon side down onto the cloth. Press with a warm iron until the colors transfer to the cloth. Then show the children the bedtime blanket. Keep the blanket in the classroom as a reminder of the Bible story. (Remember, if you write words on the drawings they will transfer backwards onto the cloth.)

Blanket Roll-ups

GET LIST:

Fruit leather
Paper plates
Markers

On each plate, draw a simple little boy figure. **This is Samuel.** Introduce the children to Samuel on their plates. Then hand each child a fruit leather snack. Tell them this is Samuel's bedtime blanket. Have them unroll their blankets and put them on Samuel. When they are finished tucking Samuel into bed, remind them of how Samuel heard God calling his name. Tell them they can talk to God too, just like Samuel did. As they eat, encourage them to talk to God. *Be aware of children who may have food allergies.*

Hearing Sounds

GET LIST:

Empty film canisters

Various small items, such as rice or dried beans

Duct tape

Fill each canister with a different item, which will make different sounds. Check all small items with a choke tube first. Then seal them carefully with duct tape. Talk to the children about Samuel and how he kept hearing his name being called. He wondered where the sound was coming from. Have the children shake the canisters and listen for the different sounds. See if they can guess what is inside making the sound. Remind them it was God who was calling Samuel and Samuel talked to God. Encourage them to talk to God just like Samuel did.

Sleepy Samuel

GET LIST:

Assorted blankets

Assorted pillows

In the Bible story, Samuel was in bed when he heard the voice of God calling his name. Have the children pretend to be sleeping. Then call out their names, in loud and soft tones. Remind the children they can pray and talk to God just like Samuel did. Let them know that God is always ready to listen to their prayers.

Loud Prayers, Soft Prayers

GET LIST:

Old telephones or cell phones

Picture of Jesus

Praying is simply talking to God. Set the picture of Jesus out so that all the children can see it. Have the children use the phones to talk to Jesus, or simply have them go up to the picture and talk to him as if he were really there (surprise, he is!). Have them practice by repeating simple prayers. Have them say these prayers by repeating after you in loud and soft voices.

Thank you, Jesus, for my _____.

Let me tell you all about when _____.

I love you because _____.

I want you to know _____.

Weaving Blankets

GET LIST:

Hole puncher
Colored index cards
Yarn
Scissors
Tape

Punch 12 holes around each index card. Cut the yarn into two-foot lengths. Tape one end of the yarn to the index card. On the other end, wrap tape around the end of the yarn so that it makes a needle-like point that can be used for threading the yarn through the holes. Have the children thread in and out or up and down through the holes. They can try to thread some of the cards together to form a "blanket." As they work, remind them of the events which happened in the Bible story.

Praying, Praying

GET LIST:

No supplies needed

Sing to the tune of, "Hurry, Hurry, Drive the Fire Truck."

Praying, praying, in the morning,

Praying, praying in the morning.

Praying, praying in the morning

Tell God everything.

Repeat using these other verses:

Praying, praying, in the daytime.

Praying, praying, in the nighttime.

Praying, praying, in the bathtub.

Praying, praying, for each other.

Praying, praying, while I'm playing. (Nice tongue twister!)

Talk to God

GET LIST:

No supplies needed

Use this simple rhyme to remind the children that they can talk to God at any time. You might want to add simple arm movements representing the time of day, and ending with flexing muscles for might.

Talk to God in the morning.

Talk to God throughout the night.

Talk to God in the daytime.

Talk to God with all your might.

Who's Under the Blanket?

GET LIST:

Small lightweight blanket
CD player
CD
Masking tape

Use the masking tape to make a small circle on the floor. Have the children stand on the circle. Have someone help you stretch the blanket out over a part of the circle, over the heads of the children. Tell the children as the music starts they are to walk around the circle. When the music stops, the blanket will come down on whoever is standing under it. Play the music. Encourage the children to keep moving to the music. Then, stop the music. Ask, **Who's under the blanket?** Then say, **Is Samuel under the blanket?** Then have the children shout out the name or names of the child or children who are under the blanket.

Samuel Talks to God

GET LIST:

Bible Story Pictures for Lesson 6 (pages 56-57)
Pillow
Blanket

Call a child over to a quiet corner. Invite him or her to snuggle up for a bedtime story using the pillow and the blanket. Show the Bible story bed as you tell the Bible story. Ask the child to help you look under the story flaps. Encourage the child to talk to God before returning to play.

Tell God about everything. (Philippians 4:6)

GET LIST:

Bible
Puppet

Hold up the Bible for the children to see. Let them know that the Bible says, "Tell God about everything." Bring out the puppet. Introduce the puppet to the children. Have the puppet whisper in your ear. Tell the children the puppet has something important to tell them. Have the puppet say, **Tell God about everything.** Ask the children to repeat what the puppet said. Then show the children how they can make a puppet mouth with their hands. Have them practice saying what the puppet told them, "Tell God about everything." After you finish, let the children use the puppet too. Remind the children they can tell God everything just like Samuel did.

BIBLE TRUTH: I can pray to God.

BIBLE VERSE: Tell God about everything. (Philippians 4:6)

BIBLE STORY: Samuel Talks to God. (1 Samuel 3:1–4:1)

GODPRINT: Prayerfulness

Children love to talk, and during the toddler months they become little chatterboxes. Their language development expands rapidly during the toddler months. This is the perfect time to focus on praying. Prayer is simply talking to God. It's communicating with God by expressing our thoughts, feelings and wishes. Praying is interaction with God. What a tremendous foundation of faith you will lay for your child when you teach him or her to talk to God at all times and to tell God about everything.

T-Time with God

There are two activities that can be expressed as T-time with God. One is to set a table for two. Fill two teacups with your child's favorite beverage. You might wish to add a cookie or cracker. Have your child sit down and have a little tea with God. If you join in teatime, remember this is a time to model how everyone talks to God.

The second activity is to use two plastic golf balls and golf clubs for T-time with God. Have your child pretend to be playing golf with God. As your child plays, encourage him or her to talk to God. If you join in playing, remember this is a time for you to model how everyone talks to God.

Prayer Blanket

Use a special blanket that will not be slept with, but set aside just for its intended purpose. Use photos of friends, family and other people you want to pray for. Place the photos in plastic buttons. Attach the buttons to the blanket. Introduce the family to the prayer blanket. Talk about how the blanket will remind you to pray for the people who are on the blanket. This can be a powerful tool as you model family prayer time as well. Always keep extra buttons on hand to write in special prayer requests and for other additions to the prayer blanket.

If you pray, your child will pray. Remember praying is not just bowing our heads and folding our hands. Mealtime prayers and bedtime prayers are very important, but so are the little chitchats with God throughout your day. Show your child how you talk to God about everything and anytime.

God Is with Me

All about God and Me: To know God is to know he is always with me. Even through the tough times, I can have hope because I know I'm going through it with God right beside me.

Have no fear, God is near! This is the message your little ones need to hear!

Just as God was with Moses through dangerous and turbulent times, God is with us, too. Teach your little ones that God is with us and keeps us in his safe harbor of love. Some little ones in your care have already experienced pain, suffering, loss, loneliness and great fears. It may seem like a contradiction to say, "God will keep you safe," when bad things have happened. The safety God brings is for our soul, an eternal perspective. In the realities of today's hurts and pains, we can find immediate comfort and hope in the fact that we are never alone. We never face our troubles alone because God is always with us, through the good and the bad times.

Through these activities, show the children that in the rough times they can find hope as they remember the story of the baby in the basket boat.

Bible Truth:
God keeps me safe.

Bible Verse:
He will keep me safe. (Psalm 27:5)

Bible Story:
Moses Floats.
(Exodus 2:1–10)

Godprint:
Hope

"At Home in the Faith" Parent Reproducible p. 70

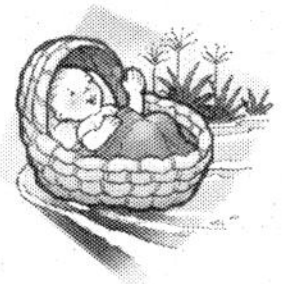

Moses Floats

GET LIST:

Copies of Bible Story Pictures for Lesson 7

Colored pencils or markers

Scissors

Glue

Color the illustrations. Cut around the outside of the Bible story booklet. Then cut apart on the heavy line. Cut out the boat figures on pages 2 and 3 in the booklet. Turn the pieces so the blank side faces you. Place the piece with pictures 3 and 4 on top of the other one. Glue the center pieces together. Fold page 4 toward you. Glue the back of page 4 to the middle piece. Fold page 3 toward you, over page 4. Then fold page 2 toward you, over page 3. Finally, fold page 1 toward you, and the booklet is complete. Page through the booklet to make sure the boats line up. You should be able to see the boat on page 4 beginning on page 2. Begin reading the story on page 1.

Read the story as you show each picture.

Picture 1:

This is baby Moses. He is in danger.

Picture 2:

God is with Moses. God keeps Moses safe in the basket boat. God is with you, too!

Picture 3:

Baby Moses floats down the river in the basket boat. The boat rocks and tips and it bangs against the rocks.

Picture 4:

His mother loves him very much. She puts him in a basket boat to protect him. She asks God to keep Moses safe.

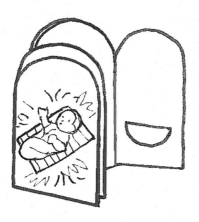

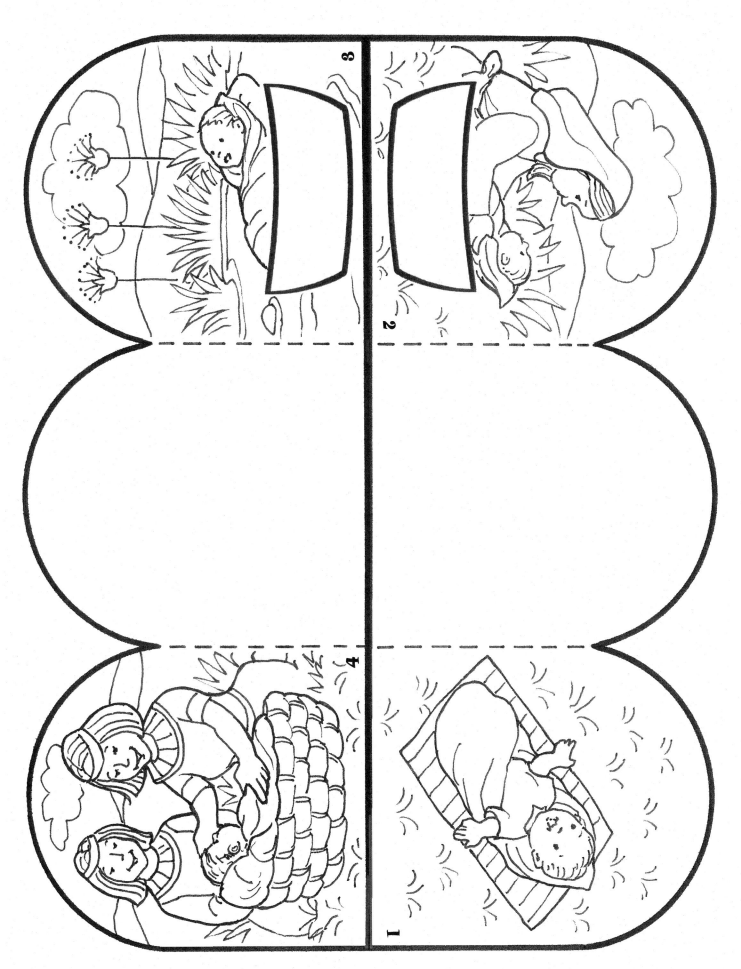

Jump the River

GET LIST:

Large blue tarp or blanket

Spread the tarp out on the floor. Turn the tarp into a river by scrunching it up so parts of the river are smaller than others. Then tell the children about how God kept Moses safe when he floated down a river in a basket boat. Show the children the tarp and tell them it is a river. Challenge the children to jump over the river. As they jump they can shout, "God will keep me safe."

Floating Baby Boat

GET LIST:

Cupcake liners
Green Easter grass
Glue
Crayons
Cotton swabs
Copies of baby Moses
Scissors

Make copies of baby Moses and cut them out. Tell the children they are going to make a baby Moses boat. Have them color the baby Moses. Hand out the cupcake liners. This is their baby Moses boat. Then help the children glue grass to the outside of their baby boats. You can help by painting the outside with glue using the cotton swabs. The children can then press the grass onto the glue areas. Then have the children place the baby Moses into their boats. Their boats will remind them of the Bible story.

Basket Boat

GET LIST:

English muffin
Peanut butter
Cream cheese
Jelly
Bear-shaped graham crackers
Craft sticks
Spoon
Toaster

Be aware of children who may have food allergies. Toast the English muffins. Tell the children they will be making a basket boat for Moses. Spoon onto their basket boats the toppings of their choice: peanut butter, cream cheese, jelly or any combination of the three. Let the children spread the toppings with their craft sticks. Then have the children add Moses, the bear-shaped graham cracker, to their basket boats. As the children make their Moses boats, remind them of the events from the Bible story.

Float Moses

GET LIST:

Tub of water

Hay or straw

Twine

Tarp or towels

Plastic people
figures

You will use straw to make little basket boats. Gather a handful of straw. Use the twine to tie both ends of the bunch. "Sculpt" the straw by pulling a little out from the middle to create a pocket. Place the little straw boat in the water. Let the children try to float the people on the boats. Tell the children about how Moses floated down a river in a basket boat. God took care of Moses and God will take care of them too.

Moses in the Basket Boat

GET LIST:

Different baskets

Dolls

Blue blanket or
towel

Lay the blanket or towel down on the floor; this will be the river. Show the children the baskets. Tell them how the baskets remind you of baby Moses. Explain how God kept Moses safe when he floated down a river in a basket boat. Let the children play with the dolls and the baskets. Encourage them to place the dolls in the basket and pretend they are floating down the river. Talk about how Moses' mother tried to protect him and took good care of him. Moses' mother knew God would keep Moses safe. Remind them that God will keep them safe too.

Sink or Float

GET LIST:

Tub of water

A variety of
different items,
some that will sink
and some that will
float

Paper towels

Tell the children that God kept Moses safe when he was in a basket boat that floated down the river. Hold up an object. Ask the children if they think the object will sink or float. Then test out their hypothesis by placing the object in the water. Repeat this process for all the items. Use the paper towels to dry off the items. When you are finished testing the items, allow time for the children to use the items to experiment on their own.

Make a Basket Boat

GET LIST:

Chenille wires

This is a free play activity where you provide the chenille wires and encourage the children to make basket boats. You might wish to build a simple model of a basket boat. You could even make a little Moses out of the chenille wires. Children can use the wires to build boats and take them apart over and over again or they could make one to take home with them. As the children work, talk about events from the Bible story. Remind them how God took good care of Moses while he was in the basket boat. Tell them that God will take good care of them, too.

I'm a Little Baby in a Boat

GET LIST:

No supplies needed

Children love to sing to familiar tunes. Encourage the children to sing this song to the tune of "I'm a Little Teapot."

I'm a little baby in a boat.

God is right with me as I float.

When I get to crying, then I say,

My God will care for me each day.

Little Baby Moses

GET LIST:

No supplies needed

Have two or three children at a time join you in a simple little poem. You might wish to add simple motions for each line.

Little baby Moses in a boat.

(Cup your hands together, rock them back and forth.)

Who is with him as he floats?

(Shrug your shoulders.)

God is with him, yes sir-ree.

(Point up and nod your head up and down.)

God is with both you and me.

(Point to the children and then to yourself.)

Foot Boats

GET LIST:

Large brown paper bags

Scissors

Masking tape

Cut off the tops of the bags halfway down. Use the masking tape to make two lines on the floor about three feet apart from each other and about ten feet long. This is a river. Place a pair of bags at one end of the river. Tell the children they're going to float down the river in their foot boats. Have the children put a "boat" (bag) on each foot. When you say, **Go**, have the children scoot in their foot boats down the river to the other end. You might wish to make this a race between two children or a relay race with children taking turns. You could have one child floating on the river at a time or make the river wider and have two or more children floating on the river at the same time. When the children finish, they can shout, "God keeps me safe."

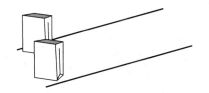

Moses Floats

GET LIST:

Bible Story Pictures (page 65) assembled into booklet

Basket

Place the Bible story booklet in a basket. Walk around the room with the basket. Hand the basket to a child. Say, **Can you tell me one thing you remember from the Bible story?** Then take the opportunity to use the Bible story booklet to retell the Bible story. Place the booklet back into the basket. Give the child the basket and tell that child to hand the basket to someone else. Whoever receives the basket is asked the question and then told the story. Continue this pattern until all the children have had a chance to carry the basket.

He will keep me safe. (Psalm 27:5)

GET LIST:

Bible

Laundry basket

Hold up the Bible for the children to see. **The Bible tells us, "God (He) will keep me safe." God kept Moses safe in a basket boat.** Point out to the children the laundry basket. Have the children pretend this is a basket boat. Invite a child to get into the basket. You might wish to push the child for a little ride in the basket boat. As you push, keep repeating the Bible memory verse. When the ride is finished, ask the child, **Who will keep you safe?** Help the child with his or her reply, "God will keep me safe."

At Home in the Faith

BIBLE TRUTH: God keeps me safe.

BIBLE VERSE: He will keep me safe. (Psalm 27:5)

BIBLE STORY: Moses Floats. (Exodus 2:1–10)

GODPRINT: Hope

There will be times your toddler experiences great fears. These may be real or imaginary. It is difficult for toddlers to distinguish between the two. The fear is there and your little one may shed real tears and experience great stress. In most cases you can wrap your arms around your child, providing a haven of safety and a harbor of love. But what if you are not around when something happens? Your little one needs to know the arms of God are always around us. Through these activities, show concrete ways God extends his arms to us.

Basket Boat

Does your child have a place to go to when feeling scared or alone? Try a laundry basket boat. Have your child sit in a laundry basket and pretend he or she is Moses in the boat. Talk about how God is with him in the boat and how God will keep him safe. When away from home, have your child close his or her eyes and picture being in the boat with God sitting right there.

Fear Busters

When a fear comes along, have God bust it! Use a permanent marker to write one of your child's fears on a balloon. You can toss and bat the balloon around. You can talk about how Moses was tossed and batted around while he was in his basket boat. Explain how God was with Moses and kept him safe. When you are finished, you can pop the balloon. Be sure to pick up all of the popped pieces of the balloon and dispose of them.

What do you do when you have a fear? Do you call on God? Do you believe God is with you through it all? Set an example for your child by explaining how you deal with fear, hurt and pain. Talk about how God has helped you through trials in your past. Give examples of how you know God was with you and kept you safe.

Follow God

All about Me and God: To know God is to know that he wants me to do what is good and right. God wants me to listen to him and follow his path. I can follow God because I know he loves and cares for me.

"Go." "Sit." "Stay here." "Don't touch that!" This is what obedience means to a toddler.

To most people, the word obedience does not stir up warm fuzzies. In most cases, the word has been clouded by too many negative human experiences. In reality, obedience should bring comfort and joy—a sense of knowing there is someone much greater than I who is in control. God has a great plan for each of us, and it includes doing what is right and good. Toddlers will soon learn that life is full of choices, not just commands. Knowing they can follow God by doing what is right and good will help them as they learn to make choices.

Through these activities, your toddlers will learn that God wants us to do what is right and good. They will also learn that we make mistakes like Jonah did, but God gives us second chances.

Bible Truth:
I can do what God wants me to do.

Bible Verse:
Do what is right and good.
(Deuteronomy 6:18)

Bible Story:
Jonah and the Giant Fish. (Jonah 1–3)

Godprint:
Obedience

"At Home in the Faith" Parent Reproducible p. 78

Jonah and the Giant Fish

GET LIST:

Bible Story Pictures for Lesson 8 copied on cardstock

Scissors

Colored pencils or markers

String or fish line

Clothespins

Optional: chairs

Color the pictures and cut out the fish figures. Hang the string or fish line near the story time area. You might wish to place two chairs back to back and tie the string from one chair to the other, leaving enough space between the chairs to hang the fish. As you tell the story, use the clothespins to hang the fish on the string. Gather the children and start telling the story with the smallest fish and continue until you finish with the largest fish.

Fish 1: **This is Jonah. God told Jonah to do what is right and good. God told Jonah to go to a city called Nineveh.**

Fish 2: **But Jonah did not listen to God. Jonah got on a boat. A big storm began to blow because Jonah did not do what was right and good.**

Fish 3: **Jonah was thrown off the boat and fell into the sea. A giant fish swallowed Jonah. But Jonah lived and the fish spat him out.**

Fish 4: **Jonah knew what he should do. He should do what God wants him to do. So Jonah went to Nineveh and did what was right and good.**

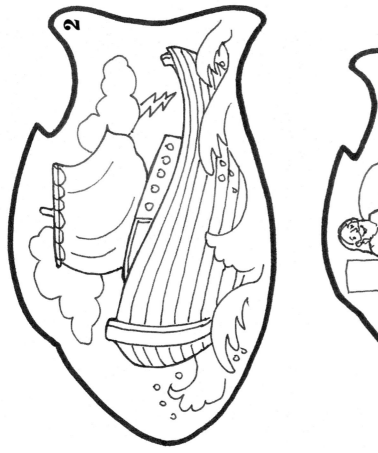

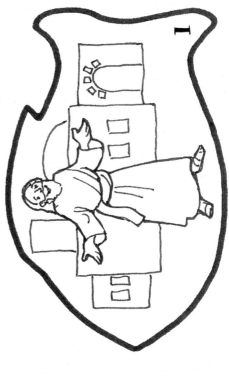

3

4

Fish Toss

GET LIST:

Beanbags
Masking tape
Construction paper
Scissors

Cut several large fish shapes from the construction paper. Use the tape to mark a large circle on the floor about five feet in diameter. Tape the fish to several spots inside the circle. The circle is a lake with fish swimming in it. The children are to stand outside the circle and toss the beanbags onto the fish. They may retrieve their beanbags and toss again from the outside of the circle. As they play talk about events that happened in the Bible story.

Sponge Fishies

GET LIST:

Small sponges
Paper plates
Tempera paint
Construction paper
Scissors

The children will be making prints of fish using sponges and paint. Put a little bit of the paint onto the paper plates. Cut the sponges into simple fish shapes and one or two small, round bubble shapes. Show the children how to dip one side of the sponge into the paint and then press it lightly onto their papers. As the children paint, share with them the story of Jonah and the giant fish. Explain how Jonah learns to follow God and do what is right and good. The fish in the pictures will remind us to follow God and do what is right and good.

Giant Fish

GET LIST:

Fish-shaped snack crackers
Paper plates
Markers
Bowls

Place the fish crackers in bowls. On each paper plate, draw a large simple outline of a fish. Hand out the plates. Have the children fill the outline of the fish on their plates with the fish crackers, or they could fill in the whole fish with the crackers. As the children eat, talk about how Jonah did not follow God and ended up in the belly of a fish. Jonah learned to follow God and do what is right and good. Encourage the children to do what is right and good. *Be aware of children who may have food allergies.*

Fishy Tales

GET LIST:

Books with pictures of fish
Magazines
Scissors

Encourage the children to explore the books and look for different pictures of fish. Point out to the children all the different colors, sizes and shapes of fish they see. If possible, cut some fish from magazines so that the children can walk with them, hold them and play with them. Then talk about the different events from the Bible story.

Fish Ahoy!

GET LIST:

Large Box
Construction paper
Markers
Tape

On the construction paper, draw a simple outline of a city. Tape the picture of the city to a wall. Cut the top off of the box. The box will be the boat. In another area of the room place the box. Have the children pretend to be Jonah and move from place to place as you retell parts of the Bible story. Start with the children near the city. Say, **God told Jonah to go to the city, but Jonah went the other way.** Have the children go to the box. **Jonah was in a boat, not at the city.** Have the children get into the boat. **Jonah fell into the water and a great big fish swallowed him.** Have the children get out of the boat. **Jonah learned to follow God. Jonah went to the city to do what was right and good.** Have the children go to the city. End the story by telling the children they can be like Jonah and do what is right and good.

Fish Puzzles

GET LIST:

Construction paper
Scissors

Use the paper to cut out large fish shapes. Then cut each fish into two- three- or four-piece puzzles. Encourage the children to take the puzzles apart and put them back together. As they play, tell them about the Bible story. Remind them that they can do what is right and good just like Jonah learned to do.

Fish Friends

GET LIST:

Colored index cards
Scissors

Cut the index cards into simple fish shapes. Try to keep the fish all the same size and shape. Make a slit in all the cards halfway down the tail from top to bottom. This will allow for the cards to be joined together. They will then stand on their own. Children can build and join together as many as they wish. They can also be easily taken apart as well. As the children play have them tell you what they remember about the Bible story.

Jonah in the Sea

GET LIST:

Construction
paper
Scissors

Use the construction paper to cut out a fish shape. Gather two or three children and sing this song to the tune of, "There's a Hole in the Middle of the Sea." As you sing the song, pass the fish from child to child.

There's Jonah in the middle of the sea.

There's Jonah in the middle of the sea.

A giant fish, a giant fish,

A fish eats Jonah in the middle of the sea.

There's Jonah in a fish in the middle of the sea.

There's Jonah in a fish in the middle of the sea.

There's a fish, there's a fish,

There's a fish who sets Jonah free in the middle of the sea.

Jonah listens to God, yes sir-ee.

Jonah listens to God, yes sir-ee.

Jonah does, does what's right.

Jonah listens to God, yes sir-ee.

I Can

GET LIST:

No supplies
needed

Call two or three children together. Say the poem several times. As you say the poem, leave out the rhyming words and see if the children can fill them in on their own.

I can do what Jonah did and do what is right.

I can listen to my God and pray at night.

I can do what is good and follow God today.

I can listen to my God and obey.

Follow God

GET LIST:

Construction paper
Scissors
Tape

Use the construction paper to cut out giant footprints. Tape the footprints to the floor around the room so that they form a line with a start and an end. **In the Bible story Jonah learned to follow God. He learned to do what was right and good.** Tell the children they can follow God too. Have them pretend they are following God's footsteps. As they step on each foot, have them say, "right" and "good." When they are finished, emphasize they can follow God and do what God wants them to do.

Tell It Again!

GET LIST:

Bible Story Pictures (pages 72-73)
Large paper clips
Tape
Pole
Magnet
String

Make a "fishing" pole. Attach the string to the pole. Attach a magnet to the other end of the string. Attach a paper clip to each of the Bible story fish. Then use a piece of tape over the clip to ensure it stays attached to each piece. Select children to come and fish for you. As they fish out a piece, read that section of the Bible story. Once all of the pieces have been fished, retell the Bible story in order.

Do what is right and good. (Deuteronomy 6:18)

GET LIST:

Bible
Soup can (unopened)

Call a child over to your area. Show the Bible. Say that the Bible says that you can "Do what is right and good." Now show the can. When you say, **I can**, have him or her roll the can on the floor as each child helps you repeat the Bible verse, "Do what is right and good." When he or she is finished, call another child over and repeat.

At Home in the Faith

BIBLE TRUTH: I can do what God wants me to do.
BIBLE VERSE: Do what is right and good. (Deuteronomy 6:18)
BIBLE STORY: Jonah and the Giant Fish. (Jonah 1–3)
GODPRINT: Obedience

Obedience can be a "fishy" subject for some people, perhaps because of distorted experiences. Shine the light of God's form of obedience on your child. God loves us and wants what is best for us. God wants us to do what is right and good, because he knows us and our future. Jonah learned his lesson the hard way by choosing not to do what God wanted. Thankfully, God is the God of second, third, fourth chances—and more! God's grace is great and so is what God wants us to do. Enjoy the activities as you discover God's way to obey.

Spin It

Have your child spin into doing what is right. You will need a paper plate, camera, tape, marker, an index card and a metal brad. Take four pictures of your child doing something right and good. Divide the paper plate into quarters. Tape each picture inside one of the quarters on the paper plate. Cut the index card to make an arrow for a spinner on the paper plate. Punch a hole in the center of the arrow and attach it to the plate using a brad. Write on the arrow, "Do what is right and good." Throughout the day pick up the plate and spin the arrow. Show your child the picture it landed on and talk about doing what is right and good.

Pancake Fish

You will need pancake batter, a griddle, syrup and a few chocolate chips. Heat up your griddle and pour a nice round pancake. Wait about fifteen seconds, then pour out a triangle tail to make a fish-shaped pancake. After you flip the pancake, place chocolate chips for fish eyes or gills. As you eat your fish pancakes, talk about how the fish reminds you of the Bible story of Jonah. Tell your child that when you see fish it reminds you of what you learned from Jonah, "to do what is right and good."

Parenting is not always easy and sometimes we blow it. We don't always do what is right and good. Remember Jonah and our God of second chances? You can do what God wants you to do. Change direction and get on the pathway to doing what is right and good.

Jesus Cares, I Care

All about God, Me and Others: Jesus cares for me and sets an example for me to care for others. He demonstrated this to me with a humble act of servanthood.

Toddlers seek unconditional love. Splash on a little love as you demonstrate by example the tender love and care Jesus has for them.

Toddlers love to watch your every movement. They will copy what you say and do. The impact you have on toddlers through your actions is significant. Jesus understood that actions speak louder than words. He set an example for us all. First he demonstrated how he loves and cares for us. Then he took it a step further and said, "Now do what I do." Toddlers will learn they are cared for and loved. Although they don't usually set out to serve others, they will take the next step to care and love others by imitating your actions towards them. They will copy what you do as you follow in the footsteps of Jesus.

Bible Truth:
Jesus cares for me and loves me.

Bible Verse:
He loved us first. (1 John 4:19)

Bible Story:
Jesus Washes the Disciples' Feet. (John 13:1–5)

Godprint:
Love

"At Home in the Faith" Parent Reproducible p. 86

Jesus Cares, I Care

Color the illustrations for the Bible Story Pictures. Cut out the feet and fold on the dotted line. Tape or glue the blank sides of the feet together to form a four-footed booklet. (Glue pages 1 and 4 to the backs of pages 3 and 2). Start by reading the story on foot number one. Then flip to the other feet as you continue reading the Bible story.

Foot 1:

This is Jesus. Jesus loves and cares for everyone.

Foot 2:

Jesus had special friends. They were called disciples.

Foot 3:

The disciples had dirty feet. Jesus showed his love by washing their feet.

Foot 4:

Jesus loves you. You can love others, just like Jesus did.

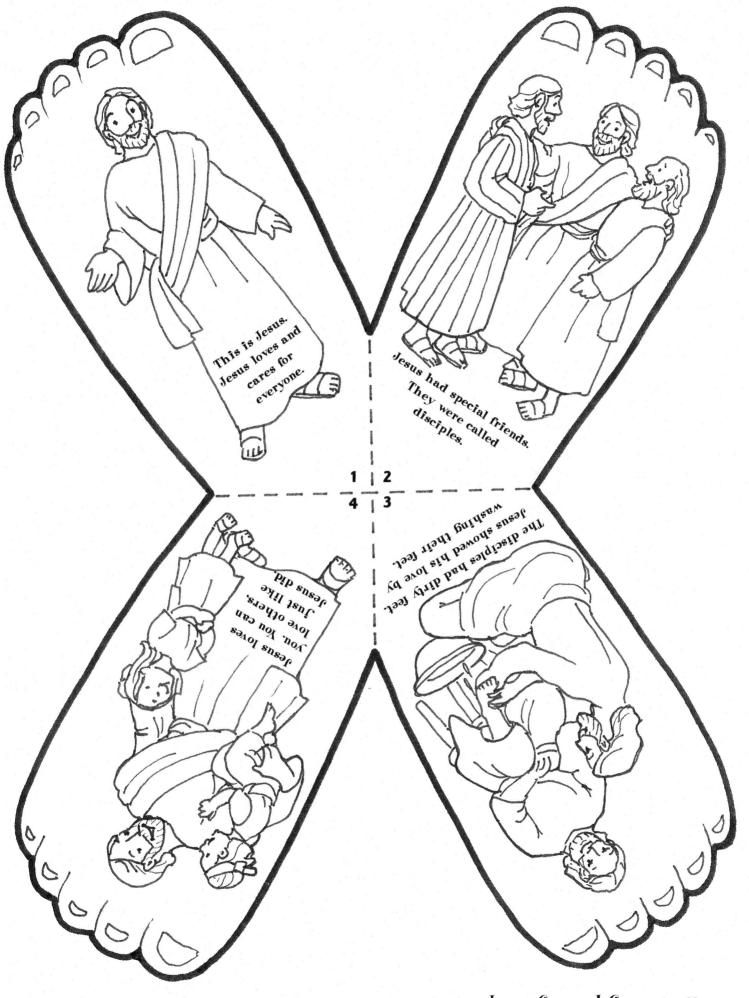

This is Jesus. Jesus loves and cares for everyone.

Jesus had special friends. They were called disciples.

The disciples had dirty feet. Jesus showed his love by washing their feet.

Jesus loves you. You can love others, just like Jesus did.

1 | 2
4 | 3

Handy Feet

GET LIST:

Toys
Toy bin or box

Say, **In the Bible story we learn that Jesus shows others he loves and cares for them by cleaning their feet. We can show others we love and care for them too.** Spread the toys out on the floor. Have the children help each other pick up toys by using their handy feet. Emphasize that we show others we love and care for them when we help them. Jesus is happy when we show others we love and care for them. Encourage children to pick up toys and put them in the toy bin or box by only using their feet.

Painting Feet

GET LIST:

Tempera paints
Stir stick
Liquid dish soap
9" x 9" dish
Construction paper
Tub of warm soapy water
Paper towels
Newspaper

This activity is sure to make a lasting impression. Pour some paint into the pan and add a squirt of dish soap; stir together. The dish soap makes for easy clean up later. Spread the newspaper on the floor and place the construction paper on top of it. Call the children over one at a time. Help remove one shoe and sock. Explain how children are going to paint using their feet. Have them dip their feet into the paint and then onto the construction paper. They can do this several times. Using their feet should remind them of how Jesus showed others how he loved them when he washed their feet. When they are finished, wash their feet with the warm soapy water and dry with paper towels. This will be a fun activity for most children. Encourage children to participate. Beware of children who may be sensitive about exposing or doing anything tactile with their feet. Some children may need time to first watch and join in later. Throughout the whole experience, show them how much you love and care for them. Express how they can show others they love and care for them too!

A Jiggly Wiggly Foot!

GET LIST:

Prepare gelatin jigglers
9" x 13" pan
Plastic knife

Prepare a large 9" x 13" pan of gelatin jigglers. The recipe appears below. Cut the gelatin into the shape of a large foot. Call the children over to look at the foot. This foot should remind them of how Jesus washed the disciples' feet. Jesus showed his love by washing feet. Jesus wants us to show others we love and care for them. Ask the children, **Do you love and care for others? If you do, then show me you love and care for others by jiggling and wiggling.** Have the children jiggle and wiggle all of their parts. Then let them eat their jiggly wiggly treats. *Be aware of children who may have food allergies.*

> **Gelatin Jigglers**
> 2 1/2 cups boiling water
> 4 3-ounce packages of gelatin
> Stir two cups cups boiling water (do not add cold water) into four packages (four-serving size) of gelatin in bowl. Stir for at least three minutes until dissolved. Pour into 9" x 13" pan. Refrigerate for three hours until firm.

Splish Splash

GET LIST:

Tub of warm water

Different shapes and sizes of bar soap

Paper towels

Beach towel

Lay the beach towel down and place the tub of water on top of it. Allow the children time to play in the water using the different soaps. Remind them that Jesus washed his disciples' feet. This was one way Jesus showed others he loved them. As children play, talk about ways they can show others love by using kind words, hugging and by being helpful.

Jesus Washes Us with Love

GET LIST:

Disinfectant wipes

Scissors

The children will be washing items in the room. If you have a dramatic play area, you might wish to have them wash only items in that area. Explain that Jesus showed his love to others by washing the disciples' feet. Let children know that Jesus loves them, too. Hand out disinfectant wipes. Have the children wash a little love onto toys and items around the room. As the children use the wipes, have them say, "Jesus washes us with love." If you wish to get really creative, you can cut the wipes into the shape of feet.

Matching Feet

GET LIST:

Construction paper

Markers

Scissors

Use the markers and the construction paper to trace the children's feet. You may do this with shoes on or off. Then cut out the shapes of their feet. Write children's names on the bottom of their feet shapes. Then spread all of the feet out on the floor. Have the children try to match their feet up. If you use different colored paper for different children, they can match size and colors too. Tell them that their feet remind you of the feet Jesus washed. Jesus loves and cares for them, just like he loved and cared for his disciples when he washed their feet.

Bubbles of Care

GET LIST:

Bubbles with wand

Before you begin, help the children remove their shoes. Children will be very excited to see you bring out the bubbles. Have the children sit on the floor. Tell the children bubbles are made by using soap. This reminds you of how Jesus washed the disciples' feet to show how he loved and cared for them. Explain that you will blow some bubbles and they will use their feet to pop the bubbles. When they pop a bubble, they can shout, "Jesus cares."

Jesus Loves and He Cares for Me.

GET LIST:

No supplies needed

Sing these words to the tune of "Take Me Out to the Ball Game." You can sing the words through twice while singing the tune once, or just pick up the tune in the middle (at "For it's root, root, root for the home team") and sing to the end.

> **Jesus loves and he cares for me.**
>
> **He loves me more than I know**
>
> **For he loves, loves, loves me so much**
>
> **From my head to my toes.**

The Toes Knows!

GET LIST:

No supplies needed

This activity requires that you or the children take your shoes and socks off. Be aware that some children have sensitive feet and don't like taking off their shoes and socks, and with some children you will have a hard time getting the shoes and socks back on. Have fun as you wiggle toes and point them out with this rhyme.

(Point to the child's big and toe and see if he or she can wiggle it.)

What does this big toe know? That Jesus loves you so.

(Point to the child's little toe and see if he or she can wiggle it.)

What does this little guy see? That Jesus cares for you and me.

Tossing Love and Care

GET LIST:

Towel
Bars of soap
Masking tape

Set the towel on the floor. Show the children the towel and a bar of soap. Tell them the towel and soap reminds you of things Jesus used to wash and dry the disciples' feet. Jesus did this to show his love. Have the children step away from the towel. Let them try to toss the bar of soap so that it will land on the towel. As they toss, they can shout, " Jesus loves and cares for me."

Jesus Cares, I Care

GET LIST:

Clean long sock
Bible Story Picture (page 82) assembled into booklet

Put the Bible story foot booklet down into the sock. Swing the sock around and around in the air. Then shout, **Who wants me to "sock" it to you?** Then gently toss the sock across the room. Have a child retrieve it for you. Ask him or her to remove the contents of the sock. Have the child help you retell the Bible story. Then put the Bible story booklet into the sock. Either you can sock it to someone or have the child sock it to one of his or her friends.

He loved us first. (1 John 4:19)

GET LIST:

Red construction paper
Scissors

Cut out the largest heart possible from the construction paper. Then cut out the center of the heart, making it large enough to frame a child's face. Walk around the room with the heart. Say, **The Bible tells us, "He loved us first."** Then put the heart in front of the child's face. Now say, **He loved _____** (fill in the child's name) **first.** Then move to the next child and repeat. Be sure to include all the children.

At Home in the Faith

BiBLe TRUTH: Jesus cares for me and loves me.
BiBLe VeRSe: He loved us first. (1 John 4:19)
BiBLe STORY: Jesus Washes the Disciples' Feet. (John 13: 1–5)
GODPRiNT: Love

How do we know Jesus loves us? Jesus has demonstrated his love to us in many different ways. The Bible story your child learned about today tells how Jesus used a simple act of washing feet to show his love and care which is extended to us. However, the story did not stop with Jesus humbly cleaning feet. Jesus gives us an example of how we should love and care for others. You are the most powerful teacher in your child's life, because it is your actions that your little one will mimic. If you follow Jesus' example by demonstrating love and care toward others, your child will follow in your footsteps and will in turn love and care for others, too.

Love BY THe FOOT

Jesus uses what seems to be a simple act of washing feet to demonstrate a powerful message. Try a few of these simple ideas expressing love by the foot. Be like Jesus and clean some feet. Have everyone sit on the edge of the bathtub, with shoes and socks off and their pant legs pulled up. Have a great time together as you wash each others' feet. You might wish to get toe...tally crazy by painting toenails and finishing off with lotion and a massage.

SHOE BOX Love

Love and care toward others is not only in what we say, but in what we do. Here is a simple way to have your child learn to show love and care toward others. As a family, choose a neighbor, a friend or someone you know in the hospital or nursing home. Take a trip to a local department store. Have your child help you purchase needed items that will fill a shoebox. This will be a great opportunity for your child to learn to focus on what others need, want or desire. At home, fill an empty shoebox with the goodies you purchased. Wrap up the box and have your child make a special delivery to the person.

When people feel loved, then they have what it takes to extend their love to others. It's a simple analogy, but think of love like a bank account. If there is money in your bank account, you can spend that money on others. If you make deposits of love into your child's love account, then they can spend that love on others.

Loving Others

All about God, Me and Others: Because I know God loves me, I can love others. I know I can show my love toward others.

Toddlers have the ability to show compassion, they just don't always recognize when to do so.

Compassion is love in action. Children at this age do not always recognize when other children or adults are in emotional or physical pain, but they can be taught the appropriate actions in response to someone needing compassion. In the Bible story, the children will see how a man needed help. His friends did more than tell him kind words. The friends helped the man. This action is an expression of love for each other, a deep love. Through the example in the Bible story toddlers will begin to see how they, too, can love each other deeply.

Through these activities, toddlers will be able to practice and learn different ways to show others love.

Bible Truth:
I can show others love.

Bible Verse:
Love each other deeply. (1 Peter 1:22)

Bible Story:
Rooftop Love. (Mark 2:3–12)

Godprint:
Compassion

"At Home in the Faith" Parent Reproducible p. 94

Rooftop Love

Color and cut out the house, the man and Jesus. Fold on the lines indicated. You will tell this story as you act it out using the house, the man and Jesus.

(Show the children the man folded into a kneeling position.) **This man cannot walk; he sits on a mat. He wants to go see Jesus, but he needs help.** (Set up the house with Jesus in the house. Point out Jesus to the children.)

His friends love the man on the mat and come to help. (Pop the friends up on the roof.)

The friends cut a hole in the roof and lower the man on the mat into the house.

(As you lower the man, unfold him so that he stands straight up.) **In the house, the man on the mat sees Jesus. He jumps up and rolls up his mat. He is healed.**

The man loves his friends and thanks his friends for helping him. (Have the man outside the house looking at his friends.)

This story is about friends who help and love each other.

Cut out

Rooftop Drop

GET LIST:

Large box with
a top

Scissors

Tossing item such
as a beanbag or
small ball

Optional: marker,
construction
paper, tape

Cut a large hole in the top of the box. You might wish to use construction paper to decorate the box so that it looks like a house. Use the marker to draw a heart on the tossing item. Remind the children how friends helped a man who could not walk when they lowered him into the house through the roof so he could see Jesus. Show the children how they can toss a little love—the item with the heart on it—down through the roof. Talk about how friends show their love to others. Add a little more excitement to the activity if you have steps available. Then have the children toss "down" into the roof from different heights.

Heart to Heart

GET LIST:

Construction
paper

Glue

Markers

Scissors

Before class, cut out hearts in different shapes and sizes. Cut enough for each child to have several. Talk about different ways friends show love. Tell children about how the friends in the Bible story show love by helping a man who sat on a mat because he could not walk. Hand out a piece of paper. Tell the children this is a mat. The mat will remind them of the friend who needed help. Help the children glue hearts onto a mat. On their mats write, "I can show others I love them." Then talk about ways they can show love to others.

Love Roll-ups

GET LIST:

Tortillas

Peanut butter or
cream cheese

Jelly

Large craft sticks

Spoon

Paper plates

Be aware of children who may have food allergies. As you call the children over to the table, hand them a tortilla on a plate. Spoon some peanut butter or cream cheese onto the tortilla. Let the children spread a little love (peanut butter/cream cheese) on the tortilla using the craft stick. Tell them how friends love to spread love to their friends. Talk about how the friends in the Bible story helped a man who could not walk. Then spoon some jelly on their tortillas. Talk about ways they can show "sweet" love to others. You might wish to have the children roll up the tortillas when they are ready to eat them as a reminder that the man rolled up his mat because Jesus made him well.

Rough Roof

GET LIST:

Roof shingle

Chalk

Damp sponge

Lay the shingle on the table. Call the children over to the table. Ask the children if they know what the object is. Explain that it is a roof shingle; it is what covers the roof of a house. Say that it reminds you of how the friends in the Bible story helped the man by cutting a hole in the roof of the house so he could see Jesus. Then let the children draw on the shingle with the chalk. To erase their work and start over, gently wipe away the chalk with the damp sponge.

Help the Hurting

GET LIST:

Cloth and adhesive bandages

Nurse and doctor supplies

Stuffed animals or dolls

Most toddlers cannot recognize or identify the emotional wounds people suffer, but they certainly are aware of people who have physical ailments. Show the items to the children. Tell them people who are hurting need our love and help. Let them know that Jesus wants us to always show our love to our friends. Jesus wants us to help the hurting. Give the children time to play with the items. As they play, talk about ways they can show love to others. Have them practice what they might say or do with the stuffed animals or dolls.

Ways to Show Love

GET LIST

Cube-shaped box

Copy paper

Markers

Tape

Large coin

In this activity, a pair of children will be able to practice ways to show love with each other. Before class, cut out four paper hearts. Cover the flat sides of the large coin with paper. On one side, write the number 1. On the other side, write the number 2. To make the "show love box," tape a square of paper to each side of the box. Then write the following words or draw a corresponding picture for each word on each side of the box: hug, smile, handshake, thumbs-up, high five, give your heart. This activity requires two children playing with you at the same time. Have one toss the "show love box" in the air and the other flip the coin in the air. Then have each child do what the toss and flip indicates. For example, if you toss "shake hands" and flip "2," have the children shake hands two times. As you play, tell the children how friends can show their love to each other, just like the friends in the Bible story showed their love. Every time they toss and flip, shout out, **How can you show love?** Respond with the ways they can show love as determined by the toss of the box and the flip of the coin.

Building a Rooftop

GET LIST:

Blocks

Little plastic people

Flat pieces of cardboard

Provide the blocks and the plastic people for the children to play. Encourage them to build a house. Then show them how they can use pieces of cardboard to build roofs on their houses. Have them use the little plastic people to act out the Bible story. Remind them of how the friends helped the man who could not walk. Tell them about how they helped him down through the roof of a house so he could see Jesus.

The Friends on the Roof

GET LIST:

No supplies needed

Sing this song to the tune of "The Farmer in the Dell."

The friends on the roof.

The friends on the roof.

They show their love and kindness.

The friends on the roof.

The friends help the man.

The friends help the man.

They show their love and kindness.

The friends help the man.

You can help your friends.

You can help your friends.

Show your love and kindness.

You can help your friends.

Show Someone You Love Them

GET LIST:

No supplies needed

Children need to practice the skill of showing others love and kindness. Toddlers will have fun in this little rhyming exercise. Gather the children together and have them stand by each other. Say the rhyme. Then tell the children to find someone and shake hands. Say the rhyme again. Now tell the children to find a different person. This time have the children give a hug. The children will catch on fast as to when to stand and when to "find" someone. Continue saying the rhyme and having the children show different ways to be warm and kind. Examples of actions to do: give a high five, thumbs-up, give a smile, pat on the back, say "I love you." When the activity is finished, remind children they can be warm and kind to others.

I can show someone I love them by being warm and kind.

I can show someone I love them; they won't be hard to find.

Mat Roll-up

GET LIST:

Two beach towels
Masking tape

Use the masking tape to make a two-foot square on the floor. Lay the beach towels on the floor equal distance, about one foot, away from the square. Point to the beach towel and tell children these are their mats. Have two children sit on the mats. Say that the mats remind you of the mat the man had in the Bible story. He sat on a mat because he could not walk. Then when the man saw Jesus because his friends helped him, he no longer needed the mat. He rolled up his mat and walked home. Have the children stand up and roll up their mats. Have them carry their mats to their home, inside the square. Try to see how fast the children can pick up their mats and carry them home.

Rooftop Love

GET LIST:

Bible Story
Pictures house
(pages 88-89)

Use the Bible story house to retell the Bible story to individual children or to small groups of two or three children. Let the children show you how the Bible story house works. As you tell the story, have older children help you decide what happens next in the Bible story. When you are finished with the story, ask the children to tell you how they can help their friends.

Love each other deeply. (1 Peter 1:22)

GET LIST:

Bible
Large foam cup
Scissors
Red construction paper
Drinking straw
Tape

Make a pop-up surprise. Cut a two-inch heart out of the construction paper. Tape the heart to one end of the straw. Cut a small hole in the bottom of the cup. Insert the straw down into the hole so the heart disappears into the cup. Hold up the Bible for the children to see. Tell them, **The Bible tells us to "love each other deeply."** Show them the cup with the heart inside the cup. Then pop the heart up. **What does this heart remind you of?** Tell them, it reminds you of love. Have the children repeat, "Love each other" when the heart shows. Then pull the heart down. Ask the children, **Where did the heart go?** Tell them it went deep into the cup. Have them say, "deeply" when the heart is deep inside the cup. Repeat the phrases as you pop up and pull down the heart.

Title: Loving Others

Bible Truth: I can show others love.

Bible Verse: Love each other deeply. (1 Peter 1:22)

Bible Story: Rooftop Love. (Mark 2:3–12)

GodPrint: Compassion

Although young children are quite often accused of being self-centered, they do jump at the occasion to participate in family life and in helping others. Whenever you see your child naturally express kindness and compassion toward others, point it out. For most children, practicing this skill will begin by watching you at home. Your child will learn by watching how you respond and treat others with kindness and compassion.

Slip into Kindness

You will need an old pair of slippers that everyone in the house can wear. Put the slippers in a place where everyone is sure to see them. Make an announcement that as a family, you're going to be looking for people who show kindness and compassion toward others. Start by giving an example. You might say, **The other day, I caught _____ slipping into kindness when _____ did (or said) to _____.** Then have the person you selected as the example wear the slippers for a lap around the house while everyone cheers him or her on.

Refrigerator Friends

Showing compassion to others begins with how we treat our friends. Fill your refrigerator door with pictures of your family friends and your child's friends. These are the people that your child will be certain to have interactions with. Throughout the day, ask your child, "Who is your friend?" Then have him or her point out or tell you a friend's name. Then say, "How are you going to show your friend kindness?" Have your child demonstrate with you how to show kindness to the friend. You will see the fruits of compassion when you practice these skills with your child.

As parents, we tend to be very quick to point out the mistakes our children make. Be just as quick to point out the great things your child does, like showing others kindness and compassion. It truly is a trait worth celebrating, so shout it out from the rooftop!

God's Family

All about God, Me and Others: To know God is to know that I belong to him and to his family. I belong to a larger group of people, and we are all brothers and sisters in the family of God.

Toddlers know about human families; it is the first group they belong to. Welcome them into God's heavenly family.

Zacchaeus was not liked by many people. He was lonely and did not fit into any group. Now most toddlers really don't mind being alone. They really don't occupy themselves with "fitting in"—yet. Most people will spend their lifetime trying to "fit in." If only everyone could have the privilege of being in your class where they'll learn there is no need for searching or climbing trees. You can be part of the grandest family of all, God's family. Welcome your little ones into the everlasting family tree!

Through these activities, your toddlers will learn that they belong to the greatest family of all, God's family.

Bible Truth:
I belong to God's family.

Bible Verse:
We are children of God. (1 John 3:2)

Bible Story:
Zacchaeus in Jesus' Family Tree. (Luke 19:1–10)

Godprint:
Belonging

"At Home in the Faith" Parent Reproducible p. 102

Zacchaeus in Jesus' Family Tree

GET LIST:

Bible Story
Pictures for
Lesson 11 copied
on cardstock

Colored pencils
or markers

Scissors

Tape

Craft stick

Color the tree, Jesus and Zacchaeus figures and cut them out. You may add a craft stick to the back of Zacchaeus to make him sturdier. For the tree and Jesus, fold the tabs back on the dotted lines to form a stand. Cut the slits on the base. Hook the tabs together on each figure to make the tree and Jesus stand. Cut the solid line in the center of the tree. Insert the Zacchaeus figure in the center slit toward the bottom of the tree.

Show the children the tree and introduce them to Zacchaeus. Tell the story:

Zacchaeus was a tiny little man.

Zacchaeus did not have many friends. He was lonely.

He climbed up a tree so he could see.

(Slide Zacchaeus up into the tree.)

Now Zacchaeus could see way up high in the tree.

Do you know what he saw?

He saw Jesus. (Bring out Jesus and stand him by the tree.)

And Jesus looked up in the tree and saw Zacchaeus.

Jesus told Zacchaeus to come down from the tree.

Zacchaeus came down the tree. (Slide Zacchaeus down the tree.)

Jesus told Zacchaeus he wanted to be friends.

Zacchaeus was so happy he jumped up and down.

(Slide Zacchaeus up and down.)

In fact, Jesus told Zacchaeus he loved him.

Now Zacchaeus is part of Jesus' family.

(Have all the children jump up and down.)

Jesus loves you too! You are part of Jesus' family too!

(Have all the children jump up and down.)

Climbing Trees

GET LIST:
Masking tape

Use the tape to draw out a giant tree with branches on the floor. Point out the tree to the children. Tell them Zacchaeus met Jesus when he was in a tree. Children can climb or jump from branch to branch. As they play, remind them of the events from the Bible story.

Jesus' Family Tree

GET LIST:
Copy paper
Markers
Scissors
Potted tree or tree branch
Yarn or ribbon
Hole punch

Before class, use the copy paper to cut out enough leaves for each child to have one. Tell the children they're going to help you make Jesus' family tree. Let them know Jesus wants them to be in his family, just like he wanted Zacchaeus to be in his family. Hand out the leaves. Let the children color on the leaves. Write each child's name on a leaf. Punch a hole in the leaf. Loop a piece of yarn or ribbon through the hole. Have the child hang the leaf on the tree. As they hang the leaf say,
_____ (child's name) **belongs to Jesus.**

Cupcake Trees

GET LIST:
Cake mix
Ice cream cones (flat bottoms)
White frosting
Green food coloring
Plates
Bowls
Craft sticks or plastic knives

Before class, prepare the trees. Mix cake mix according to instructions on the box. Put the ice cream cones in a muffin tin or on a cookie sheet. Fill the ice cream cones three-fourths full of the cake mix. Bake at 350° for 15–20 minutes or until the tops spring back when touched. Put the white frosting in bowls and add several drops of green food coloring. Have the children spread the frosting on the treetops. As they prepare and eat their snack, remind them they are in Jesus' family tree, just like Zacchaeus. *Be aware of children who may have food allergies.*

Leaf Rubbings

GET LIST:

Various artificial or real leaves from trees

Copy paper

Chalk

Tape

Scissors

Tape the leaves to the tabletop. When you call the children over to the table, tell them how the leaves remind you of the tree Zacchaeus climbed. Tell them how Zacchaeus became part of Jesus' family. Let them know they are part of Jesus' family too. Show the children how to place the copy paper over the leaf. Then rub the side of the chalk over the paper to make the leaf appear. When the children are finished, you might wish to cut the leaves out and hang them on the Jesus' family tree.

Zacchaeus' Family Tree House

GET LIST:

Large Box

Call the children over to the dramatic play area. Tell them about how Jesus and Zacchaeus met. Then tell them Jesus went to Zacchaeus' house because now Zacchaeus was part of Jesus' family. Show the children the box house. Have them pretend this is a tree house. Encourage the children to invite each other into Jesus' family tree house.

Opposites Attract

GET LIST

Different sized magnets (not too small)

In the Bible story are many opportunities to talk about opposites. As the children play with the magnets, point out opposites by using questions or directions. For example: **Point to the magnet that is (near/far). Touch the magnet that is the (smallest/tallest). Show me a magnet that is (high/low). Which magnet is the (biggest/smallest)?** Talk about how Zacchaeus was a little man and had to climb a big tree so that he could see Jesus. Then tell them how Jesus saw Zacchaeus and told him he belonged to Jesus' family. Remind them they belong to Jesus' family too.

Class Tree

GET LIST:

Brown and green construction paper

Talk about how Zacchaeus was a little man. He needed to climb a tree so that he could see Jesus. Spread the papers on the floor. Tell the children they can use the papers to make a tree. Help them start the tree by placing the brown paper in a row on the floor. Talk about how the brown paper could be the trunk of the tree. Then talk about how the green paper can be the top of the tree. When the children are finished, invite them by name to the class's family tree.

There Once Was a Man Named Zacchaeus

GET LIST:

No supplies needed

Sing a song about the little man in the tree. Sing to the tune of, "The Wheels on the Bus."

There once was a man named Zacchaeus, Zacchaeus, Zacchaeus

There once was a man named Zacchaeus, a wee little man was he.

He climbed up in a sycamore tree, sycamore tree, sycamore tree.

He climbed up in a sycamore tree, to see what he could see.

He saw Jesus walking by, walking by, walking by.

He saw Jesus walking by, Zacchaeus jumped for joy.

Jesus made him family, family, family.

Jesus made him family, a happy little man was he.

God's Family Tree

GET LIST:

No supplies needed

Gather the children. Tell them they will be helping you make God's family tree. Have them spread out and sit down on the floor. Walk among the children, saying the rhyme aloud. Select one child and say, _____(child's name), **welcome to God's family tree.** Have that child join hands with you. Now walk around the room together. Repeat the rhyme aloud. Continue to repeat the rhyme until all the children are part of the "God's family tree."

Jesus loves you and me.

Welcome to God's family tree.

Welcome to the Family Tree

GET LIST:

CD Player
CD
Masking tape

Use the tape to mark a circle on the floor about six feet in diameter. Then mark a smaller circle inside the first one about two feet in diameter. Invite all the children to stand on the outer circle. Tell them when the music plays to walk around the circle. Then, when the music stops, have them all move into the center circle, with their hands in the air making a big tree. Then have everyone shout, "Welcome to the family tree." Start over by playing the music and walking around the outer circle.

Tell It Again!

GET LIST:

Bible Story
Pictures tree
(pages 96-97)

As you walk around the room, stop and ask the children, **Are you part of God's family?** Wait for a response. Then tell them about Zacchaeus. Talk about how he was a man who wanted to be in God's family. Show them the Bible story tree. Invite them to use the Bible story tree as you tell the Bible story. When you are finished telling the Bible story, ask, **Are you part of God's family?** Then shout out, **Yes, _____** (child's name) **is part of God's family.**

We are children of God. (1 John 3:2)

GET LIST:

Bible

Hold up the Bible for the children to see. Tell them, **This is the Bible, God's Word. The Bible says, "We are children of God."** Then say, **Who are children of God?** Have the children shout out, "We are children of God." Every time the children shout out, hold up the Bible and have the children point to themselves. Continue to shout back and forth.

BIBLE TRUTH: I belong to God's family.

BIBLE VERSE: We are children of God. (1 John 3:2)

BIBLE STORY: Zacchaeus in Jesus' Family Tree. (Luke 19:1–10)

GODPRINT: Belonging

A toddler's whole world is his or her family. That is all they know. They really don't recognize nor do they place any importance in belonging to other groups yet. Developmentally, this comes at a later stage in life, and how they handle it in the future depends in part on how "belonging to a family" is handled as a toddler. Give them strong roots in feeling warmth and care within the family. Provide them with daily nourishment from God's Word. Firmly plant them in the truth of knowing they are children of God. This will give them the ultimate sense of belonging, to your family and to the tree of life, God's family.

FAMILY TREE

Introduce your children to a rich heritage that lies within every family. There are many ways to display a family tree. The key is to have it on display somewhere in your house where it can be seen every day. Toddlers will love to look at the pictures and hear about family stories. A fun way to display family pictures is on an actual potted or artificial tree in your house. You can place family pictures in picture-framed ornaments. This makes a great conversation piece when people come to visit. Be sure to add a picture of Jesus to your family tree.

TREE TAG

The Bible story of Zacchaeus has many activities that include trees. Take your child outside in the yard or to the park for a game of tree tag. The idea of the game is to run from tree to tree and not get tagged. Choose someone to be "It." Then start with everyone "hugging" a tree. The person who is "It" shouts out, "Hug God's family tree." Then everyone runs to a different tree and tries not to get tagged. Continue to play for as long as you wish.

When it is good to be part of a human family, imagine how great it will be to be part of a heavenly family.

Helping Hands

All about God, Me and Others: To know God is to know he will help me at anytime because he loves me. Because I'm secure in knowing I will receive help from God, I can help others. I know God wants me to help others.

Messy hands, busy hands ... toddlers need practice with their helping hands.

Toddlers are usually eager to help—for the first five seconds. Toddlers need lots of practice in using their helping hands, especially when it comes to helping each other. Provide them with plenty of opportunities to help each other. They need to know that God can use them to help others.

Through these activities, toddlers will learn that there are lots of ways to use their helping hands.

Bible Truth:
God wants me to help others.

Bible Verse:
We must help the weak. (Acts 20:35)

Bible Story:
Ruth Helps Naomi. (Ruth 1—4)

Godprint:
Helpfulness

"At Home in the Faith" Parent Reproducible p. 110

Ruth Helps Naomi

GET LIST:

Bible Story Pictures for Lesson 12 on cardstock

Colored pencils or markers

Scissors

Tape

Color the pictures and cut out the figure on the solid lines. Fold back where the hands connect. Fold back the tab at the edge. Fold the rectangles forward on the dotted lines. Tape the tab to the back of the first hand to form a pop-up in the round. Gather the children. Read the story starting with the picture of Naomi, then Ruth, and finally the two of them together.

Hand 1: **This is Naomi. She is an old lady. She had no one to help her. She is all alone.**

Hand 2: **This is Ruth. She is a young lady who loves God. She wants to use her helping hands to help Naomi.**

Hand 3: **Ruth helps Naomi by picking up grain in the fields. They used the grain to make bread. Because of Ruth's helping hands, they are both happy. God wants us to help others, too!**

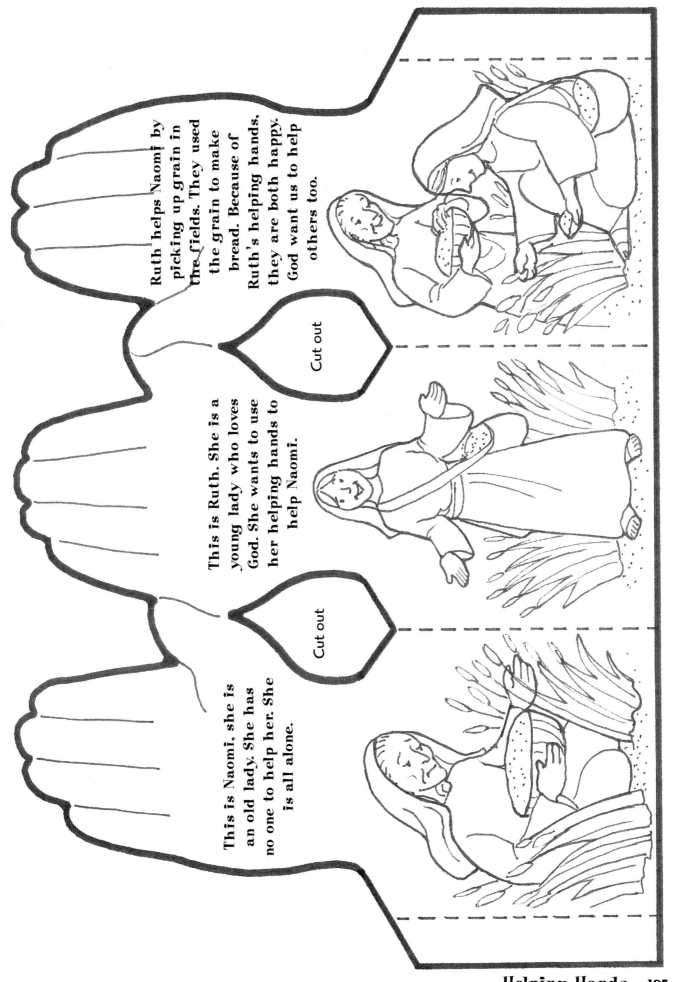

Ruth helps Naomi by picking up grain in the fields. They used the grain to make bread. Because of Ruth's helping hands, they are both happy. God want us to help others too.

Cut out

This is Ruth. She is a young lady who loves God. She wants to use her helping hands to help Naomi.

Cut out

This is Naomi, she is an old lady. She has no one to help her. She is all alone.

Gathering Grain

GET LIST:

Colored craft sticks

Brown lunch bags

Spread the craft sticks all over the floor. The craft sticks are pieces of grain. In the Bible story, Ruth gathered grain to help an old woman. Tell the children they can be helpers too. They can help pick up grain just like Ruth did. Hand out the lunch bags. Use the bags as baskets to help each other gather up all of the grain. God wants us to help others, just like Ruth helped Naomi.

Grain Pictures

GET LIST:

Colored dry noodles

Glue

Construction paper

Show the children the noodles. Pretend the noodles are grain. The grain can be a reminder of the grain that Ruth collected for the old woman, Naomi. Ruth was a good helper. Tell them they can be good helpers too. Hand out the construction paper. Help the children glue the grain onto their papers. When they are finished, tell them their pictures will help them remember to be good helpers just like Ruth was a good helper to Naomi.

Stalks of Grain

GET LIST:

Pretzel rods

Canned cheese spread

Paper plates

Ruth gathered different kinds of grains so she and Naomi would have food to eat. Ruth was a big helper for Naomi. Have the children pretend the pretzels are stalks of grain. Place all the pretzels on one plate. Have the children help each other serve the "stalks of grain" (pretzels). Let the children carefully pass the plate around to each other. As they pass the plate they can say together, "God wants me to help others." You can add a squirt of cheese to the plates of children who want to dip pretzels. *Be aware of children who may have food allergies.*

Pick Up the Grain

GET LIST:

Two bags of multicolored mini marshmallows

One bag of white mini marshmallows

Tub

Mix all the marshmallows together in the tub. Be sure to monitor this activity closely, as little ones tend to want to eat the marshmallows, squish them or lick their fingers. Explain how Ruth had a very hard job to do. She had to pick up grain every day. She did this to help Naomi. The children can be helpers too. They can help each other find the "grain"—the white marshmallows hidden in the "grain field." They can help each other just like Ruth helped Naomi. God wants us to help each other. You might wish to turn this into a sorting activity as well. The children could sort for the different colors of "grains" in the "grain field."

Serving Others

GET LIST:

Serving trays

Plastic dishware

Serving others is one way to help others. Ruth served Naomi by gathering food. We can serve others too. Show the children the serving trays. Explain that these are serving trays. Let the children know they can use the trays to help serve each other. When they serve each other, have them say, "God wants us to help others," and have them say, "Thank you," when they have been served.

Counting Grain

GET LIST:

Paper plate

30 index cards

Metal brad

Scissors

Markers

Hole punch

Cut the index cards into oval shapes. Use the marker to divide the paper plate into quarters. Number each quarter section on the plate from 1 to 4; include dots with the number too. Cut one of the index cards into an arrow. Punch a hole in the center of the arrow. Attach the arrow to the center of the paper plate with the metal brad. This is a spinner.

Spread the oval shapes—pieces of grain—on the floor. Have the children take turns spinning the spinner. The number they land on indicates how many pieces of grain they get to gather. Play until all the grain has been gathered and then begin again. As you play, talk about events from the Bible story.

Helping Hands

GET LIST:

Blocks or other construction materials

Different sizes and kinds of gloves

Ruth used her helping hands to gather grain for her old friend Naomi. Show the gloves to the children. Have the children put on some helping hands. Have them use their helping hands as they build. As the children work, talk about events that happened in the Bible story.

Clapping Hands

GET LIST:

No supplies needed

Join the children together. Sing the song through one time to the tune of "Jingle Bells." Then have the children join you in singing. As they sing, have them clap hands, then pound hands together by making two fists. Then have all the children join hands for the last two lines.

Clapping hands, pounding hands,

Joining hands to help.

Others need to follow us

In helping out our friends.

These Are Helping Hands

GET LIST:

No supplies needed

Gather the children to say this simple rhyme together. You might wish to add the actions to the rhyme.

These are my helping hands; they're as helpful as can be. (Open hands stretched out front.)

These are my working hands (pounding), **they're happy as you see.** (Wiggle fingers.)

God wants me to use my hands to help each other out. (Swing your arms.)

I can use my helping hands to help and clean and shout! (Have the children raise their hands in the air as they shout.)

Toss a Helping Hand

GET LIST:

Rubber gloves
(beware of latex allergies)

Stuffing material such as rice, popcorn, packing peanuts

Twist ties

Masking tape

Construction paper

Scissors

Marker

Trace your hand on the paper. Cut out about five or six hands. Use the tape to make a three-foot circle. Tape the five or six hands to the floor inside the circle. Stuff the gloves with material and tightly tie off the bottom of the glove. Have the children stand on the outside of the circle. Have them toss the gloves onto the circle hands. As they play, talk about ways they can use their helping hands.

Ruth Helps Naomi

GET LIST:

Bible Story Picture hands (page 105)

As you walk through the room, shout out, **"Give each other a helping hand."** Have all the children stop what they are doing and join hands. Then read one of the pages from the Bible story hands. Then let the children go back to playing. After a while, shout out, **"Give each other a helping hand."** Have the children stop what they are doing and join hands again. Once they have all joined hands, read the next part of the story. Continue the same pattern as often as you like. They'll soon be screaming, "Give each other a helping hand."

We must help the weak. (Acts 20:35)

GET LIST:

Bible

Gather the children. Hold up the Bible for everyone to see. Show the Bible and tell them that the Bible says, "We must help the weak." Have all the children join hands in a circle. Let them know they joined hands to help each other. Then repeat the first part of the Bible verse, **"We must help."** When you say the next part, **"the weak,"** have everyone fall down to the ground. Then have the children stand back up on their feet, join hands and do it again. They will love to repeat this over and over again. The big challenge will be to have everyone continue holding hands as they fall and stand again.

BIBLE TRUTH: God wants me to help others.
BIBLE VERSE: We must help the weak. (Acts 20:35)
BIBLE STORY: Ruth Helps Naomi. (Ruth 1—4)
GODPRINT: Helpfulness

In the Bible story today the children learned about Ruth and Naomi. Ruth used her helping hands to help Naomi. Toddlers are eager to use their helping hands. Show your child how to do simple tasks. Encourage him or her to do things on his or her own, even if it's not quite right. (And don't "fix" it if it is messed up). Here are some activities to help with using our helping hands.

HELPING TO THE BEAT

Toddlers really want to help out, but their attention spans keep them from actually finishing the job. Normally a toddler's attention span is only one or two minutes long. That is actually about the length of a song. Some songs may be a little longer, but music seems to help sustain attention and task completion. As your child helps you with a task, play a song. Tell your child that he or she will only help you as long as the music is playing. When the music is finished, get permission from your child to either play another song as you both continue, or finish the job on your own.

HELPING HANDS

Trace your child's hand on a piece of paper. Cut it out. On each finger write a job your child can do to help you out. Post the hand on the refrigerator. For example, make cookies, sweep the floor, clean out the cabinet, set the table or feed an animal. Throughout the week, ask your child if he or she would like to help you out. Then have your child go to the helping hand and pick out a job to do together. Color in the finger of the choice your child gave to you. Once the hand is completely colored in, have a little celebration.

There are lots of ways for little ones to help around the house. Tell your child about times you were helpful when you were little. It's important for your child to see how you have developed and progressed in your ability to do things and help others out. Let them know their helping hands will grow someday too!

Child's name: _____ Today's Date: _____

What I Did Today

Your child had a wonderful time with More Toddlerific! Bible stories and activities.
Here's what we did today.

Dear Mom and Dad,
This is what I learned today:

Bible Story:_____

Bible Truth: _____

Comments: _____

_____

_____

Teacher's Signature:

_____

Index

Index of Topics and Bible Stories

Ark 31
Awe and Wonder 39
Baby Jesus 15
Belonging 95
Christmas 15
Compassion. 95
Disciples 79
Easter 23
Family. 95
Feet 79
Fish 71
Friends 87
Helpfulness 103
Hope 63
Jesus 15, 23, 39, 79, 87, 95
Jonah 71
Lost and Found. 47
Love 79
Moses 63

Naomi 103
Noah 31
Obedience 71
Praise 23
Prayerfulness 55
Preciousness 47
Powerful. 39
Promises 31
Resurrection 23
Rooftop 87
Ruth. 103
Samuel 55
Sea 39
Sheep 47
Shepherd. 47
Tree. 95
Trust 31
Zacchaeus. 95
Worship. 15

Index of Scripture References

Genesis 6:9—9:17 31
Exodus 2:1–10 63
Deuteronomy 6:18 71
Ruth 1—4 103
1 Samuel 3:1—4:1 55
Psalm 27:5. 63
Psalm 145:13. 31
Psalm 147:5. 39
Jonah 1—3 71
Matthew 2:1–12. 15
Matthew 27:33—28:8 23
Matthew 28:6 23

Mark 2:3–12. 87
Mark 4:35–41 39
Luke 12:24 47
Luke 15:3–7 47
Luke 19:1–10 95
John 13:1–5 79
Acts 20:35. 103
Philippians 4:6. 55
1 Peter 1:22 87
1 John 3:2. 95
1 John 4:19 79